THE
FIRST
PLAN
TO
END WAR:

TO PLAN A PEACEFUL
WORLD CIVILIZATION

******

DR. RICHARD W. KAISER

The First Plan to End War:
to Plan a Peaceful World Civilization

ISBN-13: 978-1503302174 (softcover)

Available in eBook editions from major online retailers

This book is intended to provide accurate information with regard to its subject matter; however in times of rapid change, ensuring all information provided is entirely accurate and up-to-date at all times is not always possible. Therefore, the author and publisher accept no responsibility for inaccuracies or omissions and specifically disclaim any liability, loss or risk, personal, professional or otherwise, which may be incurred as a consequence, directly or indirectly, of the use and/or application of any of the contents of this book.

CONTENTS

1 Help Wanted: One Emperor 1

2 Checks and Balances 23

3 We Begin the Search 35

4 What Should a Utopian Civilization Look Like? 45

5 Planning Details 55

6 Possible Scientific Innovations................... 85

7 Possible Scenarios 97

8 The Decade of 2180-90, 170 Years Into the Future . 101

9 The Decade 2150–2140............................. 131

10 The Decade 2120–2110............................. 145

11 The Decade 2090–2080............................. 153

12 The Period 2060–2050 159

13 From 2030 to the Present 171

14 An Agenda 211

15 The Decade 2540–50, Hell 219

About the Author.......................................223

Throughout history, wars have been started by Kings, Dictators and Emperors. This is the first time we can study a practical plan for permanent peace that may work. It will take a long time, and be almost impossibly difficult. But here they are: the tools that may rescue mankind from oblivion. Why not try to learn to use them?

The Information Revolution and the Mass-Psychology Revolution with the new social media… have unimagined potential for a better, or worse, civilization. Today, social unrest in one small city is instantly on 'Facebook' or similar media, with real-time action on TV screens everywhere. It really is a new world… where people are more concerned because they are more aware. What we lack is leaders who have the courage and foresight to use these and other new tools that are coming soon to build a world that is focused on peace.

1

HELP WANTED: ONE EMPEROR

Empire Amerika? Can we discuss it openly, or is it still a secret? We can see it all around us: the first empire in history that lacks an Emperor. And it lacks a centralized power structure…. a hierarchy. It is something huge and visible, and it has plenty of power…. an amalgamation of economic, political and military power …. and it is everywhere. Some people have called it 'The New World Order '. But it is not new and there is little order. Others say it is controlled by the secretive Bilderberg group. But it is out of control. It is world-wide, but most people call it American.

The Empire began in the 1940s with the collapse of many old empires (German, Japanese, British, French, Dutch, Belgian, et cetera) and the de-facto conquest of the world by an America that was naïve enough to permit the Russians to take nearly half of it for their private empire with Joseph Stalin as its emperor. Russia's communist economic and social system was too flawed to really defeat America, but nobody knew it then. Americans were worried and motivated to work hard.

In 1945, Western armies held back and let the Russians conquer a major portion of Germany, all of eastern Europe and Manchuria. The Russians stripped most of the industrial machines out of the partly-destroyed German factories and carted them off to Russia. These 'used' machines were once the source of the tanks and planes that had conquered much of Europe and Asia in the late 1930s... machines put in place in the 1920s and 30s. Then the US gave or loaned the Germans and Japanese the money to put in the newest machines that were much more efficient than the obsolete stuff the Russians had taken. Thus you have one facet of the German and Japanese 'economic miracle' and an inefficient Russia using thousands of obsolete machines.... eventually exhausting itself in constant competition with the West.

Did all that happen by accident?

Or, was it part of a plan?

Was it the brilliance of the American and English financiers, who needed a continuing 'enemy' to justify the huge profits they would make during the following 40-year 'Cold War'? The growth of the Anglo/American military-industrial partnership during the 1950s provided the heart of the world empire that we see today.

Many English-speaking technicians, businessmen and military personnel spread over the world to trap Russia in a ring of allies and military bases that (along with the inefficiencies of Communism) eventually caused the Russian collapse in 1989. This collapse was another great opportunity for profits as western financiers re-built the Russian state-controlled empire as private industries.

Looking again at the same 1946 period, we see the United Nations, designed by the British and Americans at the Yalta conference to be forever ineffective at preventing wars. Its General Assembly designed as a place for talking, but little action... a typical chaotic 'pure democracy' where all countries had equal power, resulting in no power to make decisions. And the all-powerful Security Council with its hands tied by the veto from any one of five countries. That had to be someone's idea.... keep most countries busy shouting while world is run quietly by the new group of insiders.... an empire without borders and without an Emperor.

The post-War business opportunities allowed many American corporations to expand internationally. They were joined by British, German, Japanese, French and other business organizations. The great banks followed, opening worldwide offices and financing projects everywhere. Soon regional stock markets were expanded to service growing international investments. The heads of these corporate, banking and finance organizations learned to work with the leaders of all governments, using English as the new world language. Eventually these business and financial groups learned to manipulate government leaders and lawmakers to benefit themselves. They joined with the military-industrial groups to form great networks of mutually supporting enterprises... and they all made tons of money. It is these networks of commercial, financial, industrial and military relationships that form today's amorphous world empire.

We now see this matrix of international organizations that are controlled by management teams reporting to many different top executives who follow independent goals for high profits, but who may also work with other organizations…. as the head of a construction company building a dam in some Asian country may work with the builders of power generators for the dam and with government officials, banks and the heads of other companies who will put in factories which will use the electricity generated by the dam.

To the people of that Asian country, it may seem that a single group of foreigners is building the dam complex and other factories….. flooding farming valleys and greatly changing their country. And often that dam group seems to have a lot of Americans in it. To the local natives (perhaps victims of prior colonialism) it is apparently one big 'empire' that is changing their world. An American Empire.

The Bilderbergers?

There may even be political or financial groups who speak for all the participants in a given area. The Bilderburg group is named after the Dutch hotel where they first met. Its secret members consist of the heads of many international firms and governments, and it may even have some plan for the continued growth of a matrix financial empire. But so far there is no apparent worldwide coordination. The only person who seems to be designated as quasi-leader of all these disparate groups is the American President… or, if he is reluctant or indisposed, leaders from Britain, Germany, France… or possibly Russia, as members of the United Nations Security Council.

However, the American President has little power or direct control over the vast economic and social impact of the 'empire'. He can attempt to influence some or

many parts … as can other world political leaders. He
may command military forces that affect parts of this
empire. All participants are seeking power and profits….
at the expense of everyone else. But there is no rudder, or
captain, steering the ship toward social goals.

It is possible that the wealthy leaders of major oil
companies, with their political and banking friends, come
closest to forming a management group for the 'matrix
empire'. One need only to look at the profits of these
firms and their banks. And we must remember: the very-
wealthy cannot stop their addiction to profit and power.
The super- rich have a different morality… the word
'greed' has little meaning. War is just another way to make
a lot of money.

The Islamic Empires

In the current vacuum of strong world leadership, at
least one other 'empire' is expanding. This is the Islamic
kingdom laid-out for all mankind in the 7th- Century holy
book, the Kor 'an. The planned Muslim religious world-
empire needs a Caliph as God-appointed king. That job
is also open. The Muslim way of life often embodies the
Sharia legal system which has its roots in 'Draconian'
legal codes written before 500 BC.

The question is: which of three possible Islamic plans
for world domination should we be watching?

There is the obvious one, the Shia Iranian dictatorship,
with the probable coming prestige of its new atom
bomb. The Iranians are already connected with the Shia
government in oil-rich Iraq. And Russian oil from the
Caspian Sea flows to Europe through Baku and other
Muslim-dominated areas which are politically close to
Iran. Under Iranian control, these lands can dominate
mid- east energy production and overwhelm divided
European countries with energy restrictions and fast-
multiplying immigrants.

It is also expected that those European Muslim immigrants, with their multiple wives and many children, can dominate the politics of many European countries within 40 years, with the potential of yet another Muslim empire controlling Europe. Russia, with its southern border wide-open to an Islamic tsunami, may be the first to fall. Do they, along with the rest of Europe, have their eyes closed? Even the brazen threats of the Muslim immigrants in Denmark to enslave the wives of their hosts does not awaken.

Then, there is the less obvious possibility that a Sunni Muslim Pakistani military dictatorship, with its fist now full with over 200 atom bombs, may wish to roll north and west... making a new empire including Taliban and Pashtun brothers in Afghanistan, the smaller and weaker Muslim countries to the north including oil-rich Kazakhstan, eventually breaking-off Muslim Sinkiang from China, and eventually re-connecting to Bangladesh via the rich valley of the Ganges River. All without ever touching Shia Iran. That should interest India! The western media seems to ignore these potentials, and the planning that probably lies behind them.

And today there is a new group of angry Sunni Muslims who are calling for more war in Syria and Iraq. Does anyone know where all this conflict is leading? It is hard to believe there is no overall plan. Could it be the super-rich Saudis... **filling Europe with desperate Muslim refugees?**

It is clear that the West lacks leadership. We can look to empires of the past for counsel and good examples. The ancient Roman Empire saw that one person was often inadequate as leader. They experimented with a Triumvirate... three emperors, but never very comfortably. Even the great Julius Caesar shared power with Pompey for awhile. However, today's new matrix form of empire is unprecedented. It is almost as if a large group of

mathematical computer models are interacting in such a
way that no one decision-point has decisive power.... no
one can win completely and no one loses much. Most of
the rich inevitably get richer and the poor usually get ......
children. The system moves on... until it may collapse in
a major war or depression. We came breathlessly close
to a full collapse in 2008.... when trillions of dollars in
government debt went into the pockets of the already rich.
It is too big to understand or predict, so no one person or
group controls it.

Our Ship Is Adrift

At a time when the American President could be
undisputed world-leader, he is not. He seems mainly
interested in increasing his own wealth and in building
a future political system that is dominated, like China,
by one party. And the world suffers greatly from lack
of leadership. All kinds of difficulties are the result:
balkanization, petty wars, war lords, organized crime,
slavery, genocide, disease, starvation, ... the list goes on.
But this decision vacuum is not just the failure of one
man or of dissonance on the part of a small group. Nor is
it all the fault of the American Congress that has been in
political grid-lock for years... with the resulting failure
to produce legislation of significance. So the United
States, the greatest power structure in the world, drifts in
incompetence, while decisions are being made regionally
and locally that may or may not benefit the world.

This Political Incompetence is the Fault of a Few Obsolete Sections of the American Constitution

In the 2008 Presidential election, the American people
were disillusioned with the complexity of the world, and
retired into an isolationist somnolence. With most of the
money, guns and political power in the world, they chose

to elect a populist nice-guy who promised nothing but
'change'..... instead of a known flag-waving war hero who
seemed to represent aggressive action. Today's leadership
indecision is what they wanted, and got.

As a result, no major policies have been changed by
the Obama administration. Bush's economic bail-out
was continued, giving major banks, corporations and
financiers huge profits at the modest cost of a few million
ruined small home-owners. Prior to the Syrian civil war,
the nicely profitable wars in other Muslim areas continued
at the low cost of a few hundred lives yearly... mostly
foreign. Few ever expected that the divided people of Iraq
could create a democracy after the iron-control of dictator
Saddam Hussain was gone. But the region has been nicely
destabilized, and continues to be a good customer for the
US arms dealers.

Health legislation passed by the American Congress
with exhaustive effort has proved faulty. Its future is
uncertain. But it certainly gives the Democrats a lock on
future elections. And the grid-locked Congress has been
paid for another several years of self-serving irrelevance.
It would almost seem that many of the 600+ people of the
American Congress have been elected to make money for
themselves, rather than to serve their nation in its time
of need. Have they forgotten the meaning of the word
'compromise'? Are Republicans and Democrats working
for separate warring countries? Do they realize they are
weakening the very concept of democracy?

The great $700-billion-annual military-industrial
behemoth rolls on, with no plan other than in protecting
its own power .... damaging some and benefiting some.
And that is the way it is... and no one dares mess with it.
In that sense, it is uniquely American. There it is, folks, the
headless American Empire! Our newest monster.

But, wait! Is that all? Do we just hang on to this
uncontrollable model of a wealth-generating machine for

the few until its inevitable collapse… since it cannot be allowed to produce only stable wealth… it must always produce more wealth, until the financial wizards can reap more profits by short-selling into a collapse or into a good cleansing war? Can nothing be done, or are we to assume the existing malaise will continue indefinitely? Isn't that the desire of the financiers? They profit most from economic instability, not from good planning. Just when will these people who are dominated by greed begin to see that if the US collapses, they too will be destroyed.

A Strong President?

On the subject of world leadership, Dr. George Friedman, in his recent best-selling book *"The Next Decade"* provides an interesting compendium of traits which a successful American president should possess, all focused on maintaining the geopolitical balance of power (and high profits) in the American Empire's favor in every region of the world:

1. "The President's task is to align threat, consequences and effort with other challenges and shape them into a coherent strategy."
2. "….manage them and lead them…. to maintain a ruthless sense of proportion while keeping the coldness of his calculation to himself."
3. "A president has to accept casualties and move on."
4. "In the face of terror, the president must convince the public that he shares their sentiments while taking actions that appear to satisfy their cravings both for security and for revenge."
5. "…. he must always convey a sense that the elimination of Islamist terrorism is possible, all the while knowing that it is not."
6. The obsessive desire to destroy terrorism can undermine… the United States strategically."

7. "A strategy designed to prevent regional
hegemony from threatening American interests
is a balance-of- power strategy. It requires an
American presence in multiple regions."

This advice is good. But what if a President will not
or cannot follow this advice. How many past Presidents
were able to show the leadership qualities called-for here?
Were they decent, but ineffective, men (Kennedy, Carter,
Bush 1 & 2)? Or cleverly deceitful and effective (Roosevelt,
Nixon)? Or trapped by events that overwhelmed them
(Wilson, Hoover, Truman, Johnson, Clinton)? Or just
lucky... (Eisenhower, Reagan).... or very smart?

Trouble is, we never know before the election how
our 'man' will respond to crisis or how he or she will lead
in times good or bad. Our political system only assures
us that he or she will be popular... at least when elected.
And (Constitutionally) over age 35 and born in America.
..... also, (probably) intelligent, good-looking on TV, quite
rich, a good speaker, with some political experience and in
good health. That sounds pretty good. But it ain't enough.

How much longer will it take for Americans to realize
that the President's job is too big for any one person? And
when that realization finally becomes inescapable, how
do we begin to build a better way to control the headless
imperial-monster we have created? A monster whose only
goal is money, not human values..... and who can only
lead us to more war.

Let me tell you. We can't.

You cannot just begin tweaking a system that has
been growing out of control for over one hundred years.
It is un- tweakable. And you can't just junk it without
risking chaos and world war. It is just too big and involves
important cultural factors that cross too many boundaries.
And we cannot continue to ignore it, because it is moving

too fast toward an unthinkable collapse... and/or a world war of extinction.

In *"The Next Decade,"* Dr. Friedman develops the theme that the United States is vulnerable in several major regions of the world, and that its leaders must reduce that vulnerability by an unending effort to maintain a balance of power... playing off different countries and factions within certain important regions so that a minimum of force and expense is necessary to prevent any one country from challenging the interests of the United States. This appears to be the main goal of American geopolitical thinking.

In another best-selling book, *"The Next 100 Years,"* Dr. Friedman discusses the possibility of war within 20 years between the United States and Russia, of another war in the period around 2045 between the US and some countries in Europe and Asia, and yet another potential armed conflict between the US and Mexican factions in areas once controlled by that neighbor. These predictions are made by examining historical trends and joining these extrapolations with social and demographic trends... and Dr. Friedman's extensive experience as an analyst... always within the framework of an American world hegemony that is expected to be vigorously defended but not extended. The term "American Empire" is used to label this model.

It is NOT stated or implied in *"The Next Decade"* that the international behavior of the United States in 'defending' its interests, (using coercion, duplicity, or even subversion as necessary to achieve American goals) may in itself be the cause of some of the predicted wars in *"The Next 100 Years."*

Also not stated is the possibility that the three predicted future wars may be quite likely, but they may not be necessary. **If we can predict them, why can't we avoid them?** .... unless we really want them to occur.

Since there are so many who profit greatly from war...
even at the risk of destroying our civilization, is now the
time to seek a plan to end war... even if it is possible?

Let's hear it For War!

Alright. Let's get a show of hands.... Everybody in favor
of more war!

Get 'em up!

Come on! Where are your hands in favor of war?
... How about you bunch of rich industrialists...
Bilderbergers... over there in the corner? Oh. Shipping
your kids off to Argentina will no longer avoid the
radioactive fallout? Pity. Have you considered sending
them to the Moon?

Well, how about you navy guys... you've got the
submarines. Hell, you can stay down for weeks ... Oh.
Yea. That old movie "On the Beach".... the submarines
couldn't stay down long enough. The radioactive 'cloud'
finally caught 'em. Tough.

You mean, nobody WANTS wars... but we get them
anyway? Sounds stupid. And we actually PLAN for them,
because they are inevitable?

Oh. Hello. Sorry... didn't see **you had your hand
raised.**

So you feel that wars do some good? Oh. You say, not
necessarily actual wars, but possible wars. Maybe very
small wars.

Well, how do you keep possible wars from becoming
actual big wars?..........

What do you mean by 'tight controls'? ... And you
can do that? ... talk with all the parties... the Joint Chiefs,
Hillary, Senate Foreign Relations, Chairmen of Lockheed
or GM, Putin, the Chinese. Wow! Even the Ayatolla?... the
Israelis? Well, sir, you are obviously not the President...
you must be his... uh, ... National Sec.... Oh. Excuse me.

Yes, sir.... we don't need names. Well, sir, with all due respect for you and the President, we just do not see any coherent foreign policy now or for the past several... Well, yes, sir, but aren't we just drifting....

Dr. Friedman's Books

Well, sir, you probably know Dr. George Friedman and his book, *The Next 100 Years*..... Yes, sir, most interesting. Now, sir, Dr. Friedman predicts a war of some kind with Russia in the next twenty years.... and another war after another 20 years. No, sir, you can't comment on such predictions. Yes. Well, sir, Dr. Friedman writes some very general statements about the United States purposely working to keep some areas unstable, in order to counter the growth of threats to American interests in that region. That suggests some kind of foreign policy that does not seem to be public knowledge. Would you care to comment on that? No? Well excuse us for asking. Perhaps we should ask Mrs. Clinton...

Now, sir, the book we are working on here is recommending substantial foreign policy changes, as well as constitutional changes, to take place over the next Century. We really do not wish to impact near-term policy... it is too sensitive. Yes, sir. Glad you agree.

De-stabilizing Policy

But, sir, when we look closely at this 'de-stabilizing'... Dr. Friedman describes it as an effort to maintain a balance of power among countries or cultures in a region... in order to limit or reduce the resources the United States must devote to that region. Yes, sir, I know you cannot comment on that, since it is not generally recognized policy. But, taking it a bit further, isn't it possible that this continuing de-stabilizing effort by the US actually increases the risk of war?... And makes people hate us?

Or, is it just another way to get the nations in a given region to continue buying weapons from America... and also to justify continued huge expenditures by the US for new weapons from its major weapons contractors.... like Lockheed? Oh. Sorry. Yes, you cannot comment.

But, sir, if this de-stabilizing is a fact, does it not appear that the US is keeping regions of the world upset mainly to benefit American weapons manufacturers?

Well, sir, please note that nothing in this book suggests any changes that will reduce weapons expenditures in the next twenty years. Nothing to worry the big contractors about. Maybe some weapons reductions, or growth limits, in one hundred years... plenty of time for the weapons people to switch to space exploration and planetary development equipment. That, sir, is why we want to have a plan. Yes, sir. You are welcome. And thank you for visiting us.

Oh. One last thing, sir. So perhaps we were wrong about America having no foreign policy. It is just hard to see.

And, sir, we were also wrong about only emperors, kings and dictators being the ones who can start wars. Looks like you can do that, too, sir.

✳ ✳ ✳ ✳ ✳

Warlike Americans

Just about everything Americans do as a nation is oriented toward war.... avoiding, preparing, fighting, re-building, planning for the next. Been doing it for all of our history.

Changing that means changing everything. Almost easier to just drop the bombs and get it over with. The 'no war ' thing is just too big!

We have watched many empires collapse during the past hundred years, and we have accommodated to that. We have dealt with chaos, depressions, earthquakes, tsunamis and other cataclysms... but, gad!... true world peace would need an entirely new world system!

You got it!

Well, OK, just how would we begin? With the Castle!

What?

The Castle

The dream... the 'Castle in the Sky' of Kafka and Malachi Martin. The impossible dream for humanity that they have been writing about since Sir Thomas More first published his book "Utopia" in 1516.... but he and John Locke stole some ideas from Aristotle, who 1800 years before that wrote about the God-given right of man for

life, liberty and the pursuit of happiness.

Oh, that. Stupid.

Right. ... However, the **American Declaration of Independence used Aristotle's exact words to frame the American democracy.**

But many Americans have forgotten those ideals in their lust for 'prosperity'... in our 'right' to suck-up the resources of the world to give us ever-larger TV screens. Especially when we can get those resources by only giving them our IOU's (paper dollars), not our gold. Have we ever got a deal! The Romans had that deal also.... while it lasted.

OK. So we want to dream about some perfect kind of world where there is no war. No need for war. No one who wants war.

That means we must remove all the reasons and causes for war. Good luck with that! The list would go clear over the horizon. And we would have nothing left of interest.... just boredom. Well, maybe a little boredom we could tolerate.

First, you'd have to eliminate all sovereign countries. One world government, but not another UN social club. No, no... not kidding! **No!** It is not insane. The Americans

got away with it when they joined their 13 colonies
and called them the United States. Yes, it took a lot of
compromise, and it was a long time ago. We know the
European Union has been working on the same idea for
decades... they are still trying to do too much, too soon.
Impatient.

Yes, we know most countries are not completely
sovereign. They have to cooperate to get along. In
some cases they are even inter-dependent... at least
economically.

Yes. It will take generations, and a lot of work.

Hitler almost succeeded in uniting (conquering) the
world, in partnership with the Japanese and others, in
World War II. Only the Americans, the Brits, the Russians
and a few others would not cooperate. Probably because
of the German language that Hitler's empire would have
brought... damn grammar was too difficult. Forget about
Japanese.

Probably would've won the war had they all spoken
English.

And then the Russians had a go at it, with world
communism. But again, the difficult Russian language....
five declensions! And the communists could not get
people to stop cheating the system. Killed millions trying.
Karl Marx simply got it wrong. People work hard for
themselves, their families and their friends, not for some
big government. Communists are still around, but today
they like to be called socialist.

Now the Islamists are having their push for world
religious/political domination through immigration
and high reproduction. But their claim on world peace
only holds up until Sunni and Shia groups start shooting
at each other. Their weird blood feud has continued
for 14 centuries. And most do not even know why.
Institutionalized intolerance?

Fact Is, No Existing Political Ideology has the Power to Guarantee World Peace

Just look at the wars of Christianity, right up to modern Ireland. It is the same everywhere you look. And the books on Utopia over the past 500 years are generally not practical. Rather than giving us a glimpse of a true world system, they focus on small problems of ethics or church policy. Utopias may be nice to think about, but they are very difficult to define.

It is the problem definition that causes the blockage. Most planning and decision-making techniques start with a careful definition of the problem.

Lacking that, they get stuck, or they go off in the wrong direction... and crash into others' plans. That's when the wars start.

However, there is one new method of planning that is specifically designed to deal with huge or impossibly complex problem definitions. (Such as, 'what should be done by the US when a great empire, like Russia or the British, collapses?')

This new planning method was developed by architects/engineers who had to design large computer information systems and other complex industrial projects where it was impossible to see all the potential problems relating to a project ahead of time. In such complex projects, making changes in 'mid-stream' to deal with newly discovered problems caused unacceptable delays and cost over-runs.

B.U.I. Defined

Whereas traditional problem definition required a linear projection of steps from the present toward some visible acceptable goal, this BUI method has you mentally jumping from the project-beginning directly to the best-possible (utopian) goal of that project. Then, you carefully define exactly what IS that best possible end-result of the project in terms of a technical description of what you desire. You may have to estimate…. attempt it several times, or even guess.

Once the utopian goal is accepted, clearly-defined and documented, a logical 'bridge' is built backward from that goal to the project's beginning in a series of carefully planned steps using looping, or iteration, to jump from the ultimate 'utopian' goal first to the nearest logical step and then backward, step by step, to the beginning (as in the diagram, below). The number of logical steps in the process may be five, ten, or more.

B.U.I. Diagram

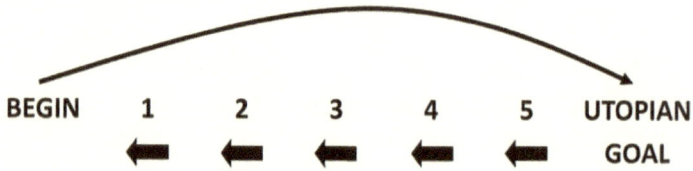

BEGIN   1   2   3   4   5   UTOPIAN GOAL

Again, you mentally jump backward from the final 'utopian' goal to the nearest check-point {or diagram step 5, above} in the direction of where you began. That step is the last one before reaching your goal……. where, from the beginning…. if you can get that far, you are almost certain to be able to reach your final utopian goal. This nearest check-point (step 5) must then be studied and its technical details carefully documented, since it is close-to, but not quite the results that you desire. And then you need to loop back to the final utopian goal to be sure you are not leaving out something important.

Continuing, you jump backward one more step {to 4} in the direction of your beginning. And, again, you study this step and document its technical details. You need to be sure that IF you can get from the beginning point to this current step {4}, you will almost certainly be able to progress further to the next-to-last step {5} and from there to the final utopian goal. And, again, you loop back (or 'iterate'… the computer term) to the next-to-last step {5} and on to the final utopian goal, to be sure you are not making mistakes or leaving something out that is important.

Yes, again you jump backward to one more step {3} in the direction of your beginning. And again you study and document this step. And again you iterate back through the steps you just did {4 & 5} to be sure you have not gone astray.

And you keep doing this {thru 2 and 1} until you actually reach your beginning point. Now, if you turn around, you will see a logical 'bridge' (all the steps) that you have created and documented from your beginning to the utopian goal that was once impossible to even define.

Of course, you can stop anywhere in the chain of steps that your current needs are satisfied.

You have now defined a best-possible (utopian) goal for your project and iterated backward from that goal to your beginning point to create a work plan.

Backward Utopian Iteration. B.U.i.

Bet you were just itching for a new acronym.

Perhaps we can use this new BUI tool to break away from the inevitable slide into war that is the result of traditional planning.

Why Bother?

It would be so much easier to just let things continue as they are. All those past empires were not so bad, except for the wars. And maybe the coming empire, when it finds a leader, will be OK. Maybe we can tweak the US Constitution a bit, force the legislators to be more responsible, and that sort of thing.

A future US president might grab the reins and bring some real direction and leadership…. perhaps even some vision… to the new empire. Of course he or she will still be controlled by the financiers, but maybe they will not be so greedy. And there will still be wars, when a region of the empire gets out of line. The endless wars of the Roman Empire all over again. And when the empire, like Rome, collapses again, we get to return to the barbarism of the 5th to 8th centuries… again. The last time that happened, we even forgot how to make concrete… for over a thousand years! Back to mud huts for most of us. Forget about schools for the kids. And disease consumed most of the world's people.

Just how many chances for a better civilization are we going to get? This is the first plan to end war in hundreds of years. Of course, it is not perfect! You need to have perfection dumped into your lap? Perhaps it is worth trying to make it work.

Back To The Castle

We get to define our utopia any way we wish…. including NO WAR. But it is not that easy. In this case our utopia is a huge system that must replace and improve our existing civilization for many centuries. All parts must be functioning in balance, as our present system is in balance except during wartime or major financial crises.

Any new system that we consider must be inherently stable and controllable by humans… correcting the weakness of the existing archaic system.

The system must meet the basic communication and control needs of our political and economic processes.

It must solve the obvious weaknesses in our present system… including over-complexity, and the tendency of human systems to periodically collapse. It must be self-monitoring and self-correcting, but it must only function within human controls.

It must create a framework for the continued growth of our civilization.

It must be adaptable to the technical needs for advanced communications and controls in an unknowable future civilization.

It must be technically feasible for implementation by normal humans within a reasonable,… say, 8 generation, time frame. And, during its development, it must protect us from war.

Its costs of development and maintenance must be justifiable and affordable.

It should be expandable into an interplanetary control system.

It must be flexible enough to accommodate to the social changes inherent in any plan to end war.

2

CHECKS AND BALANCES

Unrestrained emperors, kings and dictators usually are the ones who start wars. It is convenient to point the finger of blame at a relatively few dead leaders. But the reality of war involves much more. In the order of difficulty to stop (or head-off) a war, we can see that people can be motivated to go to war for many reasons:

on a stupid whim based on political borders and other cultural factors (World War I),
economic differences,
racial or other physical differences, and religious differences.

Often, religious wars do not end until one warring group totally destroys the other, or kills enough of the opposition to prevent reprisal. Most of the wars for the past 500 years have been of the first category: cultural or political. But since AD 600 the most prolonged wars have been religious.

People have been stopped from grabbing dictatorial power in government through the use of a political tool known as **"Checks and Balances"** that is written into a strong group of laws, which we call a Constitution.

The 'Checks and Balances' that give the United States government stability are similar to those of the constitution of the Roman Republic of around 300 BC,

... and also to the ideas proposed by the French Baron de Montesquieu in AD 1760. John and Samuel Adams used those ideas when they wrote the Massachusetts Constitution in 1779, eight years before they helped to write the United States Constitution.

The American Constitution, its amendments and historical interpretations by the Supreme Court balances the power of the President against both Congress and the Supreme Court. It gives the President the power to propose new laws, (such as a universal health care system), and to make rules to enforce existing laws. The US Congress has the exclusive right to actually write new laws, but the President can prevent a law from taking effect by refusing to approve it. And Congress can force a new law past an unwilling President by getting enough members to vote for the law. However, a minority of members of Congress who agree with the President can unite to block the majority of lawmakers, who must get two-thirds of each house of congress to vote to override an opposing President. In this series of checks, neither a President nor the Congress can usurp all the law-making power in the US government.

Most American laws originate in the US House of Representatives, which has about 425 members based on the population of states (one Rep. for about 600,000 voters). The Senate (2 members from each state) can refuse the money to finance laws that the House passes. Historically, the members of the Senate are more experienced (older) than most Representatives, and therefore Senators have a different viewpoint.

The Supreme Court has the power to declare void any new law that conflicts with those already documented in the written American Constitution, its amendments or its historical interpretations.

The US Constitution was designed to make it slow and difficult to make major changes to the basic laws of the country.

The authors of the American Constitution wrote down these complicated procedures in 1787 to prevent any one part of the government from dominating the other parts. John Adams, James Madison, Thomas Jefferson, Alexander Hamilton and Benjamin Franklin were among those writers.

They based the powers of each Senator upon the English House of Lords (stabilized around 1680 AD) and the Senate of the Roman Republic (developed between 600 and 400 BC). The powers of a member of the US House of Representatives are somewhat similar to those of an English Member of Parliament. Modern England and ancient Rome did NOT ever put their laws into a written Constitution.... the people in the ancient Roman Senate held .... and the people in the present English Parliament now hold supreme power in the land. Members of Parliament can theoretically change any law at any time, but they deeply respect the precedence of existing laws.

The United States is different. **The written US Constitution is the only supreme power in the land.** No President *or branch of Congress* can dominate the lawmaking process OR the government OR change the US Constitution. And the lifetime-secure judges of the US Supreme Court are the only guardians..... persons permitted to interpret any aspects of the written Constitution that are questioned. We all depend on their guarding well.

That the above complex Constitutional **'checks and balances'** have worked quite well for over 200 years to govern the United States is self-evident. Over 3000 years of thinking has gone into these controls. However, we must ask... are the controls adequate to govern the

American nation over the next few hundred years? And if not, what can be done to make them better?

Stability

For over 5000 years, since the earliest attempts at government by the tribes in the Nile delta, there has been a nearly constant struggle for dominance between a powerful few leaders and the rest of the population. As time passes, a king is loved, then tolerated, then resented, then eliminated. This may happen in a few months, a few years or many generations, depending on the leadership and social skills of the king.... and luck.

If a king is killed or becomes incapacitated, and if there is no obvious heir to the throne, a committee of powerful elders tries to run things for awhile (we call this an aristocracy or an oligarchy), or a group of younger people grabs control (a revolution) and tries to keep order and make decisions in a large chaotic group meeting (called a 'pure democracy') until some war or other emergency forces them to choose a new decisive leader (a dictator), who eventually takes all the power and becomes king... again.

For most of these 5000 years kings have ruled the countries of the world. But we have evidence of attempts to control the king by unhappy subjects as early as 2800 BC. In this case, a temporary 'dictator' was selected by the elders who would mobilize the defenses in wartime, and who would relinquish his power after the emergency passed. This sometimes actually happened, always depending on the personality of the leader... and luck.

The Collapse of Empires

Kingdoms consolidated into empires, and empires lasted for some centuries depending on the military skills and leadership qualities of one or a small group of persons... and luck. Thus kingdoms and empires have risen and fallen from the collapse of Sumer (around 2300 BC) to the collapse of the Soviet Union in 1989. There are always reasons to be found for the collapse of a great empire, but those reasons can usually be summarized as bad luck. It is bloody difficult to run any large enterprise over a long period, whether it be a big company or an empire. In the end, the personality of the leader is the decisive factor.... and luck.

And so today each person in the world has some vested interest in the effectiveness, the personality, of a few leaders.... and luck. What is Obama dreaming, what is Putin planning, what is German Chancellor Merkel saying, what did Clinton do? the Iranian leaders? The Chinese? Who has The Bomb? Who might use it? Who has to go and fight whom, over what? Chaos. Luck.

Good luck, and we have peace, family, comfort. Bad luck.... Hitler. Bin Laden.

But, is that the best we can do?

Is there more risk today than in previous history? Are the stakes higher, or does it just seem that the answers to problems are more obscure than before? Or perhaps the complexity of the world system has become beyond the ability of any person or group of experts (even the vaunted Bilderberg group) to understand. And we must again hope for some good luck. Because we really do not know how to control our ship of state.

History Continues to Be an Accident

It is not that a war is completely accidental. Some person had to want it, or at least wanted to risk war to get what they wanted. But it was an accident... bad luck... that person got the power to take the stupid risk that results in war. For how many more centuries must we tolerate a system based on accident? Do we have another Century before we destroy ourselves... by accident?

But there is no accident in human nature. While all people are different in some ways, groups of people react to problems or emergencies in ways that are similar, observable and predictable. A pattern of behavior can be detected over a period of time.

Everywhere we look, for all time, groups of people have sought STABILITY in their methods of government. They want only to tend to their private affairs and trust governmental decision-making to some one or group who will keep things on an even keel. They want to know what the rules are, and they do not want many changes... as long as they are left alone to pursue their own interests. But they seldom get the stability they desire.

They get kings who lead them to war to satisfy personal ambitions, aristocracies that bankrupt the society with their luxuries, legislatures whose elected members waste their time and money on corrupt practices or absurd projects. And the people have to watch in disgust as the tugging and pushing of the various factions in their government compete for power, wasting the riches of the land in the process.

Isn't this what we have today?

Over a period of 50 centuries, or 250 generations, we can observe that kings and emperors dominated all cultures most of the time. But in the brief periods when people had some say in their own government, that government was chaotic due to the unending struggle between the power of major factions.... the leadership group (king, emperor, aristocracy) that keeps most or all power to itself versus the legislatures, parliaments and other groups that want power to benefit the people. The balance of power of kings over those who they rule has been contested since the beginning of recorded history.

We need to take one glance at the roughly 40-year experiment in Athens, Greece, about 2500 years ago (450

BC) when 'pure democracy' was practiced by thousands of people gathered together shouting their opinions concerning the laws they were enacting. The system was chaotic and tended to favor groups of poorer people who wanted government handouts, but it worked for awhile because respected leaders such as Pericles were able to dominate the shouting.

Unfortunately, the more-efficient military dictatorship of Sparta eventually took control of Athens, but the brilliance of a free Athenian culture and education dominated Greek and Roman thinking for nearly 1000 years. The marble temples and monuments of Athens today give testimony of the greatness of that time, whereas there is scarcely any trace of ancient Sparta, whose mostly wooden buildings have disappeared.

The laws that the Athenians debated publicly were not new. Lists of rules, what to do and what not to do, had been made in kingdoms from before 2000 BC in Asia Minor (modern Turkey, Palestine and Iraq). Athens had a list of very harsh laws drawn up around 600 BC by a general named Draco (called Draconian laws) who got his ideas from the harsh laws chiseled into stone by king Hammurabi in Babylon some 1200 years earlier.

Around 350 BC the amazing Aristotle spent time as a paid consultant writing constitutions (customized lists of laws) for many of the Greek city-states.

The Roman Democracy

The many centuries of the Roman Empire began with emperor Augustus shortly before the birth of Christ. Before Rome became an empire, it was a kingdom from about 700 to 509 BC, and then for a paltry **482** years it was the semi- democratic Roman Republic. All power in the Republic was held by the Senate and the people of Rome. The earlier period of cruel dominance by Etruscan and Roman kings was an obsession to later Romans, and **they** designed their Republic to insure that no one person (a king or dictator) could EVER rule them again.

The Roman unwritten 'constitution' was a body of laws and Senate decisions handed down by tradition over more than 500 years. A complex series of 'checks and balances' was used in the government of the Roman Republic to prevent the leaders, who were chosen by the senate, from taking too much power. However, the Roman economy became dependent on the slaves and booty of nearly constant successful warfare as Rome expanded, and the power of generals who commanded the victorious Roman legions was nearly overwhelming.

Around 200 BC a Roman general named Sulla used his army to conquer his home city of Rome twice, and dominated the Senate as Dictator. But instead of perpetuating his rule, he retired after one year as boss, and gave power back to the Senate. A year later they cut short his retirement, with a dagger.

But the power of the Roman Senate was weakened. About 150 years later the Senate was intimidated by Julius Caesar 's magnetism and military successes. Julius was so popular as a general and dictator that he nearly became king before the Senate murdered him in 29 BC, and the ensuing ten-year civil war destroyed the Roman Republic.

The victor in the civil war, Caesar 's grand-nephew Octavian, later named emperor (Caesar) Augustus, was the first of dozens of Roman emperors. Among other things, Julius and Augustus *named two of our months.* How's *that* for power? Will we someday have a 'Bill Gates' or 'Reagan' month?

Movement of Power

The interesting aspect of the Roman Republic's history is the slow but constant movement of power from nearly complete control by the people (the Senate, part of whose members were elected by committees of citizens) to the dictatorial power of Sulla and subsequent dictators and emperors. It is a challenge to understand the complex Roman institutions that were set up **to prevent the dominance of a single ruler.** They appear primitive when compared to the sophistication of today's written American Constitution, **whose primary goal is the same…. to prevent kings and dictators.**

The point is… that both the unwritten Roman constitution and the American Constitution were designed to prevent all power falling permanently into the hands
of one person (a king). Both systems worked well for hundreds of years. The Roman system was changed greatly over time, **but it still** *failed to prevent* **an all-powerful emperor.**

It was set up as a clear and stable set of checks and balances on the use of power. But it could not change enough as the needs of the times changed, and as the success of the Roman military conquests added giant new blocks of conquered land to their country, with many disparate peoples and a huge population of slaves.

The Greek and the Roman democracies **failed** because their laws and practices of government (their Constitutions) were not flexible enough to adapt to changing needs. Or they were not strong enough to prevent the cancer of corruption.

Today's American Constitution was also designed around the principles of separation of powers discussed by Greek historian Herodotus (circa 450 BC), Aristotle's ideas of unchanging God-given personal freedom, Tacitus' record of Roman politics around the birth of Christ, John Locke's ideas of the people's right to control their leaders (circa 1750 AD), and the Baron de Montesquieu's ideas (1760) of checks and balances to prevent one part of the government from dominating the others. The American Constitution was mostly written by John Adams with much input from Madison, Jefferson, Hamilton and others. All these men had learned their history well.

The writers of the U.S. Constitution were educated men who had studied the writings of Aristotle, Locke and Montesquieu as well as those of Plato, Tacitus, Hobbes and Rousseau. These philosophers wrote about the unchanging rights of people as opposed to the dominance of kings. But most saw a 'pure democracy' (rule of the majority… as in ancient Athens) as too chaotic.

In 1787, the American writers designed their new Constitutional Republic to…

…tie the hands of the majority with the bonds of a difficult-to-change written Constitution, to protect the rights of minorities.

The Weakness of the US Constitution

They seldom agreed completely with each other. None wrote about the changing needs, desires and tolerance of the people for the controls imposed by government ….
or of the changing geopolitical and natural environment. *Therein lies one weakness of the Roman…* **and of the American Constitution.**

Another weakness: Many early American leaders owned slaves. Thus, they did not see that very cheap male labor (slaves or poor immigrants) sometimes destroys the higher civilization that uses them. (Women workers usually return to families in their homelands. Men work, remain and reproduce.) The more educated bosses often get lazy and less fertile from their luxuries, while their laborers get strong and fecund (more fertile) from their work. Sooner or later the stronger and more numerous workers enslave their masters. Today, many use poor Muslims or Latinos or machines (computers?) as their 'cheap labor '……

✳✳✳✳✳

This effort at developing a new future model government (an ideal civilization) is based on a new utopian concept. Rather than using one of the three standard prediction models (the repetition of historical cycles, historical disruption and historical trend analysis), this book will seek to define a civilization based on optimum human values and desired outcomes and to build a bridge from the present to the attainment of those goals.

3

WE BEGIN THE SEARCH

The challenges of the next two centuries will require strong governmental systems with advanced communication methods.

Once a unified World republic is achieved, many functions of existing governments will evaporate or radically change, ending the need for large and expensive government.

The programs envisioned herein seek to provide the stability that would enable human prosperity and individual freedoms, with self-discipline, to be maintained over the long term.

No governmental system now in existence would fully meet these needs.

We now begin the search for a better one.

The previous discussion on constitutional history is only one facet in the consideration of a proposed utopian system. In order to build a model of a possible utopia that may be developed over a long period we must explore further. We can only guess at the number of generations the process will take ... trying to allow enough time to clean up the mess we now have and to build improvements. Moving too fast will increase the risk of collapse and/or war. People need time to change.

Politically Oriented Religions

The problem of politically-oriented religions may take centuries to solve peacefully. The criteria for their evaluation must be their contribution to the search for world peace. The intransigence of any established religion, especially one that has a political agenda of world conquest, forces solutions that must consider religious, moral and social aspects which will take time and sensitivity to address.

The power of Islam is in the pure simplicity of the faith and in the large families that can metastasize new colonies quickly or see their children as martyrs in the conviction that they are sending them early to certain paradise. This is not the place to discuss the details of Islam or 'Sharia' law.

Western cultures may not need to change the thinking of immigrants who disagree with their values, just to limit the numbers of these angry or dangerous elements in their own countries. Most of the immigrants insist that their religion is peaceful. It may be better for them live in peace in their own homelands and among their own extended families.

The French, in their desire for empire, opened their doors to poor Algerians as citizens of European France. The Dutch and English did the same with their colonies. With their major European cities now dominated by fast-reproducing unhappy, uneducated and unemployable immigrants, the recent governmental errors have become the problem of all western nations. To allow the immigrants to remain guarantees their eventual majority, and therefore political domination.

To change this demographic certainty without civil war will be very difficult. At this time it is not 'politically correct' for western governments to openly address this problem. Many officials are intimidated and afraid of physical harm if they speak out individually. Existing liberal immigration and social laws have failed to protect them. But the problem can only become more difficult, and most of Europe will be involved. A painful and dangerous period of writing and enforcing new laws is necessary.

Cultural explosions that may dominate this Century seem certain. Hopefully, they can be kept local and brief.

The particular problem of nuclear-armed Pakistan, is too important a topic to be ignored, but too dangerous to be more than mentioned. We must assume that these dangers are being addressed by various groups in the United States government and the United Nations with close consultation with the Pakistanis.

Pakistan

Pakistan is a poor country in the dry mountains and drying Indus river basin to the west of India. Earthquakes and floods often ravage the country. The population in 1965 was about 100 million... this has grown rapidly to about 160 million today. Many countries, including Hitler's Germany have encouraged rapid population increases to prepare for conquest. In the past generation, there has been an explosion in the population of many middle-eastern nations. It is not known if there has been some plan behind this population explosion. Pakistan has exported millions of people to Europe, especially England. With a high birth rate, and a large young population, there are few jobs. Many unemployed young people are oriented toward Jihad against all infidels, especially Americans. Pakistan is very hostile to India on the east, and is heavily involved with the Pashtun tribes and Taliban politics of Afghanistan on the west. The Pashtun and related peoples are also dominant in western Pakistani border provinces.

At the time when India developed the atom bomb, with probable help from Russia, the Americans needed the cooperation of Pakistan to oppose the Soviet invasion of Afghanistan. Thus, the Americans evidently closed their eyes (with some wrist-slapping and impotent sanctions) while a very poor Pakistan developed its own atom bomb, possibly with aid funds from the Americans.

The scope required in this study of civilization cannot permit further focus on the problems of political religions and Pakistan. But they cannot be ignored.

This plan assumes the eventual success of European countries in controlling those immigrants who would dominate them, an eventual reduction in the birth-rate of dominated-women due to poverty and over-crowding in their homelands, and an eventual possibility of moderate intellectuals to de-emphasize or re-interpret the more aggressive passages in their unchangeable holy texts. With the Europeans occupied with these problems, with Russia focused on empire-rebuilding, and with east Asia economically strong but culturally fragile, the world will look to North America for leadership in the search for a world without war.

Utopia

A utopia is, according to the Encarta encyclopedia, "an ideal and perfect place or state where everyone lives in harmony and everything is for the best." It is a place where most persons may pursue happiness, within the overall rule of law, as they define it. It is not envisioned that all persons on the planet must achieve all aspects of a utopia. We seek a middle path that hopefully will satisfy nearly all. Provision for non-violent dissent must be made….. perhaps even violent dissent.

Others define a utopia as the best and happiest civilization. Further, a civilization is an organized human system with many interrelated parts. **Let's face it; we do not really know what utopia is, or if any culture can achieve it.**

One of the first clear efforts at documenting the idea of a utopia was that of Sir Thomas More (an advisor to much-married English king Henry the Eighth), who in 1516 published his book *'Utopia'*. This was a critique of the corrupt and chaotic state of politics in England and central Europe based on the near total control of the feudal society by the Roman Catholic church, where the power of the church was dependent on the power of kings, and vice versa. More's ideal society was based on non-religious sharing by all persons according to each person's need (a communist model later expanded by Karl Marx in 1848). More's writings got him beheaded by king Henry.

More's book also caused a lot of trouble. Little thought had been given to civilization in Europe during the previous 1000 years as wars and disease killed much of the population and reduced most of the survivors to poverty. One example, the Black Death (Bubonic Plague... from the fleas on rats) of 1348 swept west Asia and Europe, alone killing nearly half of the populations, especially in the polluted and rat-infested cities.

The power of the Roman church had achieved dominance over the primitive societies of Europe, eventually becoming a force that discouraged scientific inquiry and experimentation (much of which was considered heresy).

The Feudal System, a service contract between landowners (lords) and kings, brought some political stability to much of Europe after the death, in 814, of Charles the Great (Charlemagne). But the common people were bound as near-slaves to the lands they worked (the same as today in too many countries). During the next 400 years, the dominance of a wealthy land-owning nobility, the Roman church and all-powerful kings began to be threatened by the slow rise of a middle class of merchants and artisans in England, France and the Low Countries.

Around the year 1000 universities were founded in Paris, Bologna (Italy) and Alexandria to educate clerics and sons of the elite in religion and church-law.

During the following centuries, while also preserving much learning in monasteries, the Catholic church became corrupt in the support of the kings who ruled the lands.

In 1215 the nobles in England forced King John to agree to the Magna Carta, promising to be restrained by the traditional feudal laws and limiting imprisonment without trial (now called Habeas Corpus). Thus began a slow return to the rule of law (a constitution) instead of a king's whim. But the common people remained mired in misery.

In 1378, John Wycliffe, wrote his criticism of the Catholic church in England and its subservience to the Pope in Rome. Twenty years later, John Hus, in central Europe (Bohemia) echoed Wycliffe's criticisms of the church, and got himself burned at the stake by church elders... beginning a popular revolt that destroyed much of central Europe and set up its conquest by outsiders.... eventually the Hapsburgs of Vienna.

By the early 1500s gold from the Spanish colonies in the New World and increasing trade was beginning to enrich the middle classes in England and the Low Countries and incite their interest in influencing their leaders.

The utopian ideas of Sir Thomas More were published in England on the revolutionary printing presses invented by the German Johannes Gutenberg some years earlier. These presses brought to Thomas More the ideas of the Dutch philosopher Erasmus who, seven years earlier (1509) wrote *The Praise of Folly* criticizing Roman church practices and the corruption of civil law. All this came as a climate of change excited Europe over Spain's colonies in the New World.

A few years later, in 1513, an angry Martin Luther challenged the corruption of the Papal system and eventually brought down the power of the Catholic church in northern Europe and England. This in turn caused six generations of religious warfare that killed millions and again decimated central Europe ... and resulted in a flood of desperate immigrants to North America in the 16 and 17 hundreds.

But civilization is not only religious ideas.....

We have observed chaos in the historical development of political systems. We have also witnessed a thousand-year gap in the development of civilization when the Roman Empire collapsed. For the nineteen centuries between the Greek philosophers of the 4th Century BC and the re-birth (Renaissance) of the early 1500s CE few people gave much thought to personal freedom or utopia. Most were too hungry or scared.

The Islamic system delivered by Mohammed (Peace Be Upon Him) in the 7th Century AD to the impoverished tribes and desert kingdoms of the middle east was based on personal submission by all to perpetual rule by Allah and His appointed Caliph (king) and posited only a paradise after death. The desert poverty of many people in the middle-east then (and now) did not give many people the chance for happiness in life. Thus a religion that focuses on joy in the afterlife had much appeal and remarkable military success in conquering the weakened lands of the collapsed Roman and sick Persian empires.... and eventually extended eastward to the Philippine Islands. It was Islamic scholars from Alexandria (Egypt) who brought some of the ideas of the Greek Aristotle to Muslim Spain and eventually to Christian Europe.

We have neglected other great empires and cultural systems in south and east Asia, Africa, and the Americas... but we are focusing on utopian ideas. However, the remarkable peaceful accomplishments of king Ashoka (about 230 BC) in India cannot be ignored. He was arguably the greatest king in history, mainly because he stopped wars.

The smiles on the many statues of the lucky tenth-Century CE Khmer kingdom (in present-day Cambodia) shows us the essence of any utopia: happy people whose enlightened monarch kept their families fed and secure. Unfortunately, conquest by foreigners in the 1400s ended it. It did last 400 years. Looking back, we may discern that the relatively simple agrarian life of the average Khmer peasant made their happy system easier to develop and maintain. When good weather gives you bumper crops and a decent army keeps nasty invaders away life can be good indeed. However, add to that simple model a modern people's need for air conditioning, fast cars, indoor plumbing and luxury travel for all, and life becomes impossibly complex... and unstable. Utopia lost.

After the 1500s there came a flood of books on the subject of utopia.... some of them full of dreams and ideas concerning what a perfect civilization should look like. Few if any came with a clear program how mankind might reach the utopia.

Marx's *Communist Manifesto* (1848) was followed by works of Engels and others that developed extensive plans whereby workers would capture their countries via revolution and eventually yield power to a vague state ruled by worker 's councils. Installed by Lenin via revolution in 1917 Russia, the product of this plan was a ruthless dictatorship that ruled Russia and much of the world from 1919 until it collapsed in 1989.

Adolph Hitler 's book *Mein Kampf (My Struggle–1923)* writes about a world empire patterned on rigid racial German virtues which would be extended (like Islam) through conquest and power politics. But, again, the actual implementation after military conquest was left vague. While there were some idealistic points, the book mainly focused on the domination of Germany and eventually Europe. Hitler saw himself as the benevolent

'Leader ' (*der Fuehrer*) of his German 'Third Empire' utopia, but he was only another dictator.

Of the more recent efforts, the book *Brave New World* (1934) by Huxley, describes a future social system that is both fascinating and monstrous. His society depends on cloning for all reproduction, creating dangerous under-classes of resentful workers. Sex and drugs are used exclusively for recreation and population control. The system might have eventually produced a doomed race of sterile humans. Huxley's ideas excited students over the world, especially his "hot contraceptives". His political system was just another oligopoly (rule by a small group).

Behavioralist B. F. Skinner described his small utopian colony in *Walden Two (1945)*, but the cooperative mid- western village in his model needed rule only by a committee of elders, with isolation or exile as the only enforcement.... similar to the politics of the Mormons on their trek to the western US (1845), and to the primitive village in the *Epic of Gilgamesh* (about 3200 BC). Not much help in designing a future political system for a projected 4 to 5 billion educated humans.

To end this brief history of utopian ideas on a discouraging note, Robert Heinlein's brilliant novels on the future show the end result of too much programming... the god-like immortal Martians in his *"A Stranger in a Strange Land"* (1961) who preferred joint head-butting suicide to their boring eternal perfection, and the revolt of the Moon-colony in his *"The Moon is a Harsh Mistress"* (1966).

During these long centuries of gradual political, religious and social development there were also great developments in science, economics, communication and transportation. We avoid further detail on these developments in order to focus on a plan for a utopian future.

Putting it simply, a utopia is based on feelings in the heart of every person... changing with emotion, family, age, health, economy and perceived threats. It will take much time to understand all problems and design interactions, after the progression of studies of cultures, cultural histories, and intercultural differences.

4

WHAT SHOULD A UTOPIAN CIVILIZATION LOOK LIKE?

As soon as mankind progresses past the hunter-gatherer stage, work becomes the basis of all civilization, and people must learn to do work that will bring food, or money for food. Thus, education (to learn work skills) has been and remains the key to civilization. Be it farming, building or destroying, people learn to do work in order to eat, and how effectively they learn relates to the quality of their lives and to the health of their children. Education past parental training depends on some kind of human organization, called government. Effective or ineffective education determines the quality of the civilization, and that effectiveness depends on government. Other basic functions of government include settling internal disputes, defense against invasion, internal transportation, economic decisions and possibly religious leadership.

Some people can be emotion-happy under even the most difficult situations. But usually people cannot make themselves happy unless they have some protection from harm. There must be some way for each person to create an environment of satisfaction, some control of threats, some family and economic security, food, shelter and some freedom to make choices along with knowledge of likely outcomes. An ideal system would predict and correct bad choices made by each person without punishing or enslaving that person.

Also needed is a method to monitor the direction of small and large group physical movements, predict future trends in those movements and adjust education, political and economic resources to maintain a stable human environment. However, too much contentment (increasing normal human laziness) will reduce the creative problem-solving ability of people and increase the probability of system collapse.

Nevertheless, war and insurrection are not started by happy and contented people.

As a start, we must envision the interlocking but mobile parts of a really huge system.... that of a better civilization.

Assumptions

The following assumptions are basic to the development of our model of the ideal civilization we would like to see in whatever time it takes to do the job.

This model does not include any evaluation of the so- called **Disruption Theory** of the future.... *the possible end of the world system predicted in religious works,* nor on the end of civilization due to sudden apocalypse such as collision with asteroids, solar explosions or other unexpected extinction-level disasters. Human-caused disasters such as atomic war or mass starvation will be considered.

We also choose to ignore two other common methods of predicting the future. The many recent science-fiction and other predictive works based on **cyclical analysis** (a repetition of past events) or on the **linear projection of current trends** anticipate a very grim future of world war, cruel dictatorships, a society in chaos ruled by barbarians and a general collapse of civilization. The purpose of this plan is to avoid all that.

The design method we use is that which is presented in this book: Backward Utopian Iteration (BUI). Using this method **beginning with Chapter 8,** we project our thinking directly into the distant future to depict a utopian (best possible) model based on philosophical principles as related to a broad spectrum of experience. Then, in the following chapters, we will build a logical 'bridge' back to the present that may show us a practical path to that desired future.... sneakily avoiding all-out wars in the process.

The following chapters will present some details of a truly universal political system for our future utopia that is designed utilizing the present Constitution of the United States of America, with hopefully stronger 'checks and balances', with a new level of personal contact between voters and their representatives (happier voters?) and a greater distance between these (happier Representatives?) that is spanned by a perhaps overworked and unhappy computer-based Voter Information System whose job it is to do damn-near everything political you can think of.... and which is examined very closely by a group of specially-trained and well-rewarded human corruption watch-dogs.

Assumption 1: Existence

We will continue to exist, and in any conceivable utopian scheme we will have found a way to overcome or pacify all the major problems that our civilization faces today.

The question is how? And what do we mean by 'all the major problems'? That is a big order. For that reason, **this effort must invite expansion and improvement by you.**

But, that is not enough. We are seeking so much more, because there is so much more to seek. Somewhere in this mass, we must discover that body of wisdom, the sudden illumination, the spark of good luck that will show us how to achieve our objective... 'The New Castle in the sky' of author Malachi Martin.... the glistening vision of a world of human satisfaction ... that rare quality that may bring happiness to all people for a long time.... to Aristotle's dream, written 2400 years ago, of 'liberty and the pursuit of happiness' for all.... the essence of freedom.

Impossible?

There is so much to consider that the assignment of priorities must be delayed until further analysis. Carefully. Carefully. Stealing carefully from the best ideas of the past as a beginning. We must not forget that Karl Marx's written vision of a worker 's utopia he called Communism led to seventy years of pain and millions of deaths. There may be those who say that Christianity and Islam have had similar results. And, we must also consider the slow collapse of the Roman empire from many factors, which we summarize as... fatal immorality. There is danger in utopian dreams, but probable world-destruction if we continue on our present 'accidental' course of history. **Careful.... watch the stones we dislodge. We climb a ridge with an abyss on the right and left.**

For a person to be happy in a social setting, one must presume an environment that provides for basic needs and rules for all people in that setting. And that society must include a variety of work opportunities to allow different persons to find economic stability and satisfaction. Fit that group into a larger culture and one must presume some sort of formalized set of laws, a Constitution, and some sort of government to provide some balance, security and direction for the system. Subtract from this the freedom to kill each other or revolt when they are upset, and you must have a Constitution that is more responsive than usual to people's emotions. We must eliminate most or all of the reasons for war and revolt. Here you can imagine a long list of all the causes for war.... then imagine a system that eliminates each one. Without trying to do all that here, let us look at a few of the probable causes.

Political boundaries allow us pride in our little piece of ground and in our leaders.... Nationalism. And envy when the other people have ground that we see as richer, better... or just more of it. 'Let's go kill some of them.' And, of course, religious differences. ' Our god is better than their god. Let's go kill some of them.' Or we want some of their possessions.... A good example today: the oil-rich Spratley Islands in the South China Sea.... greedily claimed by China, Malaysia, Indonesia and the Philippines. We may see a war over them, or we may see a joint consortium to develop the oil field and split the oil (or the profits) by some agreed formula. Do we really need to kill somebody over this?

Now we can imagine a system where there are no boundaries to fight over, and one where anyone can go where they please and worship as they please without being coerced or attacked. And be able to live and work and be accepted everywhere in peace and harmony. Tolerance. Utopia. Of course, all this will be difficult. And it will take a plan. And the plan will have to take into account constant change in everything as we go along. And also, tribes willing to fight to the death to keep things as they have always been. We do have a long way to go.

But... if we fail in our effort to build one world... and still avoid a collapse into barbarism or a war of extinction, or yet another smothering empire; can you imagine the horrible world of the future where competing colonies on other planets are controlled by competing sections of the present world? The Americans and Chinese each own half the Moon... tugging and pushing, like two men in a single- bed. The Russians got first to Mars, and grabbed all of it. Brazil is alone trying to cool-down a bit of boiling

Venus for a dome city. The Germans and Brits are in the ice on Jupiter's moon Ganymede! India is angry at being left with only the asteroids to mine. Endless chaos and war, locked into place by our refusal to unite now.

Assumption 2: Some Tools

As we construct the parts of the utopian system in each of the areas below, there are two 'tools' which will influence the design and structure of each of the key sub-systems presented. These two factors, the most powerful societal influences since the Industrial Revolution, are the advent of Information Technology and of Mass Psychology. These tools should be used in developing all ideas.

In the time period considered, we can expect other new 'tools' to be developed, such as: new hand-held (or implantable?) language communication.... control and voting devices, revolutionary energy sources, ways to control gravity and magnetism, life-extension methods, improving the human birth and death process and the use of human thought to communicate with humans, animals and machines in possible combination with spoken language. this is only a beginning. Better monitoring of terrorist activities, weather control, coping with rising seas, population control and world pollution control will be areas of great activity. the most difficult area for improvement: governmental effectiveness.

'Singularity', the concept of computers reaching the power to exceed human intelligence, may be reached during the time span of this project. While such machines may someday rule the universe, it will take time to program or otherwise activate and load data into the monsters, and at first it may only be a toy for the super rich... who may be the first immortal hybrid human/machine 'cyborgs'.

State of the art computer network information systems will be needed for the Voter Information System... along with a communication grid that must grow from regional to world-wide. But for planning purposes we will consider innovative computing machines to be just that.... tools to be used as effectively as possible... and to be carefully controlled.

If some future computing device with super-human powers can be made small enough to implant in humans to enable unimagined multi-dimensional thought-generated communications, we will have to modify the Voter Information System to feed directly into and out of billions of these new implanted devices to provide a superior level of individualized voter and other communications, with appropriate new controls. The key to these controls would be an encrypted hard-wired (totally secure) control code that would identify every such device, along with a highly secure set of manipulative codes... and a centralized group of closely watched experts to monitor the human/hybrid system... including a team of genius teenage hackers to watch for same ... with a dedicated high-level team watching the watchers. There is danger here. Even the best of machines may be dominated by an even better machine... with the resulting slavery of mankind. We will need an 'off' button.

Any tiny electronic device that would allow centralized two-way communication with all individuals has potential to improve the quality of life for those persons. However, the potential also exists for a dictatorial government to utilized those devices to watch and control all people to suppress their freedoms. George Orwell, in his book '1984' portrayed in 1949 a horrible future world dictatorship where all freedoms were suppressed by ubiquitous electronic communication devices.

On the other hand, those same devices could better keep track of wandering (or kidnapped) children and their infirm great-great-grand-parents utilizing simple locator programming tied to files of local landmarks. It is all up to us.

Assumption 3: Universality

In the time frame chosen, we must consider all design to apply universally in the world... and to human colonies on other worlds. And all the sub-systems must also integrate into a single civilization. All these must anticipate both natural/technical 'pollution' and political sabotage..... plain human stupidity... over generations.

And, we will somehow have to convince those who now have the power to steal the world for themselves... a world empire for themselves, enslaving all others ... to remember their humanity....to let us try for The Castle. We can today see near-feudal countries that have been ruled by the iron hand of family power for centuries. Very difficult to change. Enlightenment overcomes greed only slowly.

Assumption 4: Some Tough Problems

The difficulties facing the present world civilization during the 21st and 22nd centuries are so great that it will take both wisdom and luck for humanity to traverse this period as a functioning civilization. Failure means we perish as a species or, after a war in which billions perish, we revert to some primitive or tribal state where most people are slaves. Any plan or effort we make here must consider the extreme threats posed by these and other difficulties:

21st Century: **Political religions** or near-religious political systems.

Nazi Germany under the dominance of Hitler, and the 1940s imperial Japan are examples of near-religious political systems that came close to world conquest.

Another example is the world empire of Spain under the religious Inquisition of the 1500-1800s.

Islam is an example of a **political religion** that embodies a complete political system ruled by a god-appointed Caliph and a rigid 7th- Century legal system that is imposed on all. All the world must submit to rule by religious/political leaders who use the Kor 'an... the God- given unchangeable instruction book, along with other books.

21st Century: **Global Warming.** In spite of politically induced research contradictions, sooner or later we should find out who was right. At this writing there are experts who say the earth is warming through man-made causes, warming by natural causes, and cooling.

Whatever the cause, if the oceans rise more than one foot expensive projects will be required to protect many of the world's ports and low lands. In this case, the financial and social costs of relocating or protecting coastal cities will be very great. The disruption in food supplies may cause a great reduction in world populations, but this alone will not destroy the civilization. It will certainly test us.

22nd Century: Solving the problem of a **world-language** that is part of a strong world-political union (which is probably the only way to avoid future war). Within one or two decades, hand-held devices may have both power and programming to permit simultaneous spoken language translation between two or more parties... thereby revolutionizing international relations and economics.

25th or 26th Century: **The Next Ice Age.** We do not know exactly when the cooling that will result in the next Ice Age will begin, but it will come. It could start even as the warming of the carbon dioxide buildup proceeds, since the causes of each are not related. When it begins, the radical cooling of the earth could occur over a few generations forcing a reduction in farm-lands and a chaotic movement of people to equatorial regions, under the earth surface or under the sea, that would greatly reduce the population.

We have no choice but to include in our planning some effort to counter the effects of these huge problems, and possibly others.

Assumption 5: The Ant Hill

Population control. Population held by government to levels that can be supported by each region without pollution. The right of unlimited reproduction destroys other people's right to eat. Cloning of people limits the gene pool and creates an underclass that is dangerous. Natural reproduction must be maintained, otherwise the race may become sterile (extinct), but the birth process can be made safer, easier and painless. We will find a way to take babies from the womb sooner... to limit birth pain and to improve infant and maternal survival .

Government will become more involved in child rearing. 'Lost generations' of teenage boys for any reason cannot be tolerated.

5

PLANNING DETAILS

We now begin to develop an idealistic picture of a best-possible utopian 'Castle in the Sky' that we would desire.

Our bridge from the future backward to today will be big... a superhighway at least six lanes wide, maybe more. *And the lanes must all interact and interrelate. If one fails, we all fail.* Cannot forget the abyss. A truly huge system.

Lane 1: Cultural Systems

This is the central focus of any utopian system. It is oriented toward human happiness and freedom of choice in all activities. However, human happiness is not the result of anarchy or chaos. **Human happiness is a state of mind that is controllable by each person based on individual internalized criteria and effective decision- making.** *Criteria formulation and creative problem-solving must be taught at home and in school and assisted through individual counseling.* Student age is important in this effort at self-awareness.

The concept of individual choice and freedom may be acceptable to a person with a Greco–Roman cultural heritage. This includes lands in America, Europe and the Mediterranean. Skip across the world to a village near Ulan Bator, Mongolia, and you may see a different outlook. In many eastern cultures there is less individual freedom, with an obligation to family that goes back thousands of years. In these regions, self-awareness must consider family values.

Our smug assumption of superior universal values must be examined. There is a lot of research to be done. And there is a risk that we will get bogged-down in centuries of academic disagreement, among scholars whose certainty is deadly. Compromise is difficult for persons who are convinced that only their view is correct. Academic advice in this program development must be evaluated by persons who have a broad view of life and of the project.

One of the functions of government is to create an atmosphere of family-oriented personal security for children and economic stability for adults that permits individuals to experience the satisfactions that build personal happiness. War, poverty, hunger, physical danger and slavery are to be avoided as the antithesis of happiness.

A greater understanding of human individual and group behavior must be developed, and from this effort we must learn how to improve the happiness of all people. We cannot deny the right of all humans to be individuals... to be wrong as well as right.... to test new ideas ... to change. Freedom means individual freedom. Education must match the needs of students with the needs of society. Teachers must be paid well, but must be reminded that they are being paid to teach well.

The relation between human happiness and family must be studied more. Both individual and family (children) living patterns must be supported by government policy (but not by larger government hand- outs).

In the far-distant future, the well-organized earth as a home-planet may develop a different culture from booming 'wild-west' space colonies, some of which may be producing fantastic wealth. Gold is where you find it. We have no idea what the future 'gold' will be. The earth system, coming from an embarrassingly chaotic past, may well be too stable.

While overall populations may be reduced, individual life-spans may be increased through nutrition, genetic manipulation and organ transplants.

We may eventually expect medical advances that will eliminate bacterial and viral disease, only to find that the lack of these challenges produces a weaker population. At time of writing of this book, many of the world's cultures are experiencing population reductions. With work, we may develop an optimum population plan for each region of the world based on the overall resources of that region.

The raising of children by irresponsible parents will be brought under control. Government influence will eventually discourage the birth of unwanted children. Human fertility will probably be less, making individual children too important to neglect. Single pregnant women who wish to give birth may be required to prove financial and emotional responsibility and to possibly select a willing partner from probable fathers. The state will sponsor adult training in family-building and child rearing. It will become a serious crime for parents to neglect children or to separate before children have left the home for high school (at age 13). Parental commitment will be required and monitored, but laws may recognize some parent's need for sexual variety. Happiness? Morality? Regional customs? There's an abyss to fear.

Since there may be boredom in a 'stable' existence, new forms of entertainment with strong sexual orientation and some risk may be created.

The birth process will continue to be natural, but desired conception in couples will become near 100% certain. Pregnancy terms will be reduced from 9 months, due to improvements in external incubation, hopefully without reducing fertility.

Animal cloning will be common, with some animals taking over jobs previously done by less intelligent humans or robots. The training and genetic improvement of animals will become important. Can we risk teaching a chimpanzee to speak?

To maintain an adequate human fertility rate, something will have to be done to make child-birth and rearing attractive to educated women. Fully supportive husbands might help. Child-care and governmental incentives may also help. Society needs children, but women also have a right to freedom. Until men can create children, they may have to learn to assist their wives.

Among those aged who are beyond sexual activity or other pleasant elderly pursuits, on-demand painless self-destruction may receive legal acceptance. Huxley's book 'Brave New World' envisioned all cloned persons programmed to a certain and drug-comforted death as soon as their sexual attractiveness waned... thereby excluding any of the creative thinking or leadership that older persons provide.

It may take many years even to define what are the correct social standards in a utopian world. Even our religions vacillate on the subject. Most religions posit 'peace' as the highest form of group behavior. We define peace as freedom from war, harmony between peoples, tranquility. But war has been a historically-accepted method of spreading religion. And religious wars are always the most bloody, since conquering a people does not change their religious beliefs.

Peace is often the goal of all peoples, as soon as their enemies have been defeated and enslaved. The Romans developed military tactics that were so successful their economy for 600 years was based on the booty of conquest and slave labor. And among other causes for the collapse of their empire were borders that were too distant to maintain and a huge slave population that could not be controlled.

Peace itself is a condition that is very difficult to maintain. One cause of World War I was the large groups of young European men who were itching for someone to fight. They rushed happily into a war that killed most of them. It is this human propensity for war that will take generations and much effort for mankind to understand and control. But without this effort, and without the generations of social training necessary to eliminate man's primordial instinct toward war, we will always have war. Some persons must control this training. And who will control them?

While the elimination of war as social policy is basic to a utopian society, there are other criteria to consider. Social harmony in all aspects of human intercourse is also basic to a utopia. Centuries of training may be required to control man's propensity for conflict. And, conflict reduction in humans may also affect human creativity.

A warrior class has always been an important part of any civilization, and a basic component of the political system. This class must be replaced by a group of security workers who have the potential for leadership development. Much future security work, such as monitoring and surveillance will be done with robots or other technical equipment.

A kind of social control model must be created by mankind to build a world society that is healthy and free from war. Many of these ideas are contained in the basic writings of our great religions and moral histories:

From the Dao of 4th Century BC China: **'kindness and harmony. Do not do unto people what you do not want done to you'.** Let us judge all men and all ideas by those words.

Different people have different personalities: Huxley's *Brave New World* suppresses these differences by cloning, peer pressure, mindless group sex and drug use as a horrible example of social control. We cannot ignore individual differences or the problems of overpopulation, under population, aging, education, and reproduction.

A perfect social system may produce happiness in all its people, where kindness and harmony are taught, but not bred into people (but where violent tendencies can be eliminated through genetic action and possibly diet and the elimination of dietary poisons). But if you have no aggressiveness how do you have progress? And, to what extent is 'progress' necessary?

One source gives this description of the balanced thinking of a superior human in a stable state:

'They try always to do only as much as their natural impulse requires, never straining for further achievement. they relate to other people in a spirit of natural kindness, tolerance, and humility, never striving to dominate them'. (from: Confucianism, Microsoft Encarta ® 2006.)

The *Old Testament* gives us the Ten Commandments as a set of rules and examples of exemplary living… a good beginning for any Constitution. And from the same time period (circa 500 BC), the way of Gautama Buddha shows us a tested path to serenity.

Lane 2: Moral Systems or Philosophy

In a utopia, by definition, all persons can be happy, or at least satisfied, with their lives. Huxley's *(Brave New World)* utopia uses unlimited sex and the drug 'soma' to keep most of the limited population in a state of fairly constant euphoria. And his people seem to be all below age 35. A painless ritualized and drugged death is programmed for all before advanced age. We have refused to accept this rather limited definition of happiness. Huxley's people are the product of social programming that approaches slavery. (Persons who are uncomfortable with the control process are shipped off to another region where their dissatisfaction can be 'treated', tolerated, or isolated.)

Happiness is often considered to be a state of mind, rather than a goal to be "pursued" (as in Aristotle's 'the pursuit of happiness'). And the criteria for happiness seem to be very individual and changeable. Still, there is much commonality in feelings among different people… much research to be done here. If happiness is a valid human goal, is there now any school on earth that teaches 'happiness' or 'how to attain happiness'? There are lots of schools that teach 'warfare'.

For many people the teachings of and a belief in a supreme being (a religion) provide great happiness. Others may find sadness and frustration in their inability to meet high religious standards.

In a possible utopian system, each person may have a personal written constitution in which some ideas may be modified as people change their thinking about happiness as they age. The process of learning and education should be directed at providing a young person with tools and skills to help them become effective (happy?) members of society. The rules are taught early, since most people go through a period of rebellion against rules, until they again learn to accept their wisdom.

Research can determine if people really want more sex (or more varied sex) in their lives, and in what phases (taking a few ideas from Brave New World). And human fertility and procreation must also be considered… including all moral aspects. An examination of the function of families must be made.

Many feel it is best to seek moderation and balance in all the things we do, and from that state we may discover that we are indeed happy. Many Americans (and Japanese, Europeans and others) devote too much of their time to the pursuit of wealth… or the security that wealth may bring, or the pleasure that wealth may bring. Rather than focusing on such a narrow goal, a better model may be **a balance between health, love, adequate wealth and the time to enjoy them all.**

Research will detect a statistical bell-curve of acceptable behavior in humans… society allows only a certain range of acceptable behavior in its people. Family teaching, education and social controls are used to train all persons in these behaviors. Even head-hunters are trained by parents to appreciate the finest heads for display. A control system must be designed to encourage, restrain and proscribe human behavior within the acceptable range. 'Controls'? Not like they had in Nazi Germany.

Lane 3: Political Systems

A basic political concept is that during the period of great change envisioned in the next two centuries, government will have to be strong. As world systems stabilize and enter the final phases of change the need for governmental controls will be less. As countries voluntarily join a world union (because their people will demand it), there will be less need for a large military or defense organization… and the related military-industrial complex. Imagine the threatened legions of career military officers and armament industry managers that will see their careers damaged by reduced war preparations! It will be a slow… and dangerous process.

The human tendency toward rebellion and warfare may be controlled through improved political information systems and the universal monitoring of warlike personalities in society. The question is, how do we protect the rights of those persons while we watch them? Must we try to change them?

The strange ideas of the book *"Brave New World"* may be used to promote at least the surface happiness of large groups by changing sexual mores. But the enslaving controls of the terrible world envisioned in George Orwell's book *"1984"* show us what can happen if we go too far with stifling controls.

Present countries joining to form a world union will result in fewer countries with whom to interact... which means fewer people in the business of interacting... the Departments of State. In fact, most present functions of government will disappear (for example, the US Postal Service) or be much smaller after several generations. This will upset many who now work in these fields.

With laws stable and society peaceful, legal activity will decline, the duties of a Congress will be less and the total size of government will be reduced. However, education and human services will be a large function and quite centralized, since legions of counselors and sex therapists may be needed as governmental services supporting human happiness.

As diseases are cured and prevented, the size of the medical establishment will decrease, with governmental health services focused on the aged. The size, scope and types of governmental services will change greatly over the centuries, and require careful tuning.

When solar colonies are a fact, great wealth may be coming from investments in asteroid colonies... and great risk.

a) The political changes required to avoid another world war are great. In mid-2014, **an examination of world governments reveals no country that now has the political, economic and military power and maturity necessary for leadership toward a world without war.** Without a strong commitment to a valid plan, there is little chance existing governments will purge themselves of short-sighted, greedy, childish or barbarian practices in time to avoid accidental disaster.

Among the major candidates for future world leadership, the **United Nations** was designed to be... and still is… a hopelessly weak and expensive debate club, led by a Security Council that is often deadlocked by the veto. The **European Union** is still mired in political wrangling, nationalism, monetary confusion, language idiocy and weak leaders. The **Germans** are still trying to bring order to the mess… their continuing effort to copy Napoleon over the past 160 years. The North Atlantic Treaty Organization (**NATO**) is a limited military partnership, led by the United States, that was never intended to be a government.

The **Russians,** with their dream of world communism ended, are still focusing on the same goals they had in the 18th Century…. empire-building and protection in depth by controlling nations to their south and west. They appear to be moving away from democratic government, but this may be a temporary cycle.

The **Chinese,** still ruled by an encrusted communist dictatorship that must control increasingly restless captive peoples in the north and west, have only recently begun to think beyond their treasured central kingdom, and will be occupied with internal problems and population excesses for much time. But they are ambitious, and may wish to move into space. Recent progress and continued dynamic movement in their culture requires that the Chinese participate fully in the development of future world systems. Western countries who wish to move forward must always include the Chinese and the Indian people (with some of the world's most ancient and respected societies) as principal partners in the planning process.

Japan is strong, with an ancient and respected culture, but still focused inward, except for trade. The **Muslim world (Umma)** is based upon a beautifully simple theology which has a history of growth through violent conquest, and whose basic literature has not yet been modified to be less warlike. The unchangeable words of a supreme being are nevertheless interpreted by today's leaders and scholars and given connotation or shading that can be warlike or peaceful. Aside from their beautiful theology, the political aspects of Islam are based on archaic and rigid concepts known in 6th Century Arabic kingdoms.... which have been frozen in place by their literature.

The fragments of the collapsed empires of the **British, French, Dutch, Belgian, Spanish,** et-cetera have no strength or cohesiveness. Among former colonies, the **Brazilians need** many decades to build infrastructure and solve internal problems. So do the people of **India**, especially in regard to their population problems.

So? Where do we look to find the world leaders of the future? Now, let's see.... have we considered them all? None seem to be strong enough, so far, or ready for world leadership. Are there any others to consider?... Oh, yes. The Americans.

The barbarian Americans, pulling and shoving everyone else. Stepping on toes without noticing. Like teenagers, unable to see likely consequences of their rash actions. Determined to de-stabilize all who might potentially challenge their perceived suzerainty. The America whose school kids, in the iron clutches of unionized and secure teachers, cannot find Germany on the map and never heard of Hong Kong. With tremendous economic and military power, but with a weak congress that takes many years to decide on an improved health program and wastes more than a year frothing over President Clinton's basic physical needs... not noticing political disasters elsewhere. An America so inward-looking that they may have had to sacrifice Pearl Harbor in 1941 just to notice that World War II was nearly lost.... and again the World Trade Center in 9/11 to wake-up to potential Muslim conquest. An America that would rather upset the Russians or Chinese than cooperate with them.... that chases around the globe conquering

countries as a response to a terrorist attack, and is
unaware that when you conquer a country you had better
be prepared to run it.

And yet, who else?

The Americans hire men to run their government
who have clearly vested interests in the international
oil empire, **and then they wonder why they cannot
reduce national dependence on imported oil,** ..... with
the related world expansion of the Muslim religion
supported by American oil money. Doesn't anyone see the
connection?

We also have the multinational Bilderberg group, with
the richest and most powerful people in the world who
may have a secret plan for world domination that would
secure their power for all time. A utopia for the rich...
until the next revolution. Their support of the present
world chaos is the basis for their continued power and
riches.

As of 2014, the power structure in America is too weak
to support the world leadership role that will be required
if we are to avoid future wars. The President and lawmakers are too beholden to wealthy corporations and
other pressure groups. There are too many rich Americans
who would profit from a nice little war. And they have
never learned enough history for them to see the obvious.

b) The 21st Century is going to be very difficult.
All of the stabilizing political empires of the world
have been wiped-out during the past hundred years.
But the Americans have only recently noticed that they
have created a new headless empire. In the spectrum of
governmental power, this time in history calls for more,
not less, central government control. This will reduce
some freedoms. Endlessly growing welfare programs
granted by populist legislatures can only be controlled
by responsible action by a strong executive (governor or

president). But where do we draw the line on executive power?

The time has come for us to learn more about the use of executive power in the past. We have the historical records. When will we learn from them? Records of wars and conflicts in the distant past focus on the winning side. About 2500 years ago, somehow a few Greeks stopped the Persian hoards at a place called Marathon. No, it was not just a long foot-race. It was a desperate battle. The real question should be: just how did they do it? What ideas or strategy led to their victory, and why were the superior Persians not able to prevail? About 400 years later, Julius Caesar conquered Gaul (now France).... but what was it about the Gauls that allowed themselves to be conquered by a bunch of Roman foreigners?

In World War I (1914–1918) we see that all participants were nearly equally unprepared, and the insane bloodbath that resulted held the armies in appalling fixed trenches for years. England, with the world's greatest empire, destroyed itself by feeding most of its bright young men blindly into the German machine guns in Belgium. The stupidity of their generals was beyond belief. Who let them do it? Thirty years later, in 1939, Hitler 's Germany conquered all of Europe in a few months. How could France and England have been so blind as to permit the obvious German preparations for war without themselves preparing? How could the Americans, after the battles in Europe in 1918, become so blindly isolationist as to make minimal preparation for the coming war in Europe or the Japanese attacks? It is a function of good government to keep an eye on what neighboring countries are doing. Is there no one or group in Washington today who has the mental capacity to watch all the world? And yet we are continually taken by surprise by huge international developments that upset our plans. How is it that World

War II happened at all? Do we know all those who profited from it?

We need to learn to use history to build a world society that is not so fragile. We have all the tools we need right now!

We now seem so blind to the obvious: 1. The Chinese build a large industrial base to sell goods to the Americans, and then use the profits earned to build missiles, submarines and aircraft carriers that have no use but to attack the Americans. 2. The Russian empire collapses because their governmental system could not compete with other countries, and now it is permitted by those countries to rebuild its empire through military conquest by 'insurgents' who attack one neighbor after the other. Can no one see where this is going? 3. The Americans give Middle Eastern countries trillions of dollars for their oil, and do not notice when those trillions are spent in a huge population buildup by those countries, and then tens-of- thousands of that huge population are paid to move to Europe in a conquest by immigrants of European countries that resisted Islamic military conquest three times in the past.

The leadership (executive) function in American governments needs improvement. Because the Presidency is a populist position, there is no incentive to plan for more than 8 or 10 years ahead.

Presidents are elected, but may not be well-prepared. Therefore, the presidency is essentially a training program for the first term… and then he's a 'lame duck'. As soon as he gets to know the job, he is retired into limbo. But, at least, we prevent him from becoming King. Experience for a president is provided by a few prestigious advisors whose allegiance and connections are unknown.

The U.S. Constitution needs work. The qualifications of presidents and senators are far too lax. The world can no longer afford unprepared populist leaders. Their mistakes are too expensive.

The American Constitution is a good place to begin a political system around which can be placed a social and an economic system. Given enough time, we might make a few improvements…. a very few amendments. But we certainly do not want the risks inherent in a totally new constitution.

The Present US Constitution: Articles 1 and 4

The organization and powers of Congress; the admission of new States… presently appears to permit any region or country that is acceptable to Congress as a partner State within the **Union of the United States to** be properly represented with full equality to any other member State. It would seem possible for a province of another nation, such as the Canadian province of Manitoba, to petition the American congress to join the American union as another state.

Here is a new idea that moves toward a world without any reason for war.

A great country such as Mexico would never seek to join the United States with the same status as another state, such as New Jersey or Ohio. Their perceived loss of status and sovereignty would be too great. But if that country could be confident of absolutely equal partnership at the highest level with ALL the existing American states… at the same level as the existing US constitution… the benefits of joining their country might be enough to overcome all resistance. The idea is new of voluntarily joining the United States with a foreign country (such as Canada or Mexico) and sharing equal political/economic sovereignty at the highest level. In order to do that, there must be created a new higher level of organization above the states and still under the rule of the written Constitution. This new higher group would be designed to eventually represent every region on earth and possible planetary colonies. Partial economic cooperation, as in the North American Free Trade Area with those three neighbors, is a good start. This effort may be expanded into a general cultural/economic and political union. Thus the United States may someday share power as an equal partner with other countries. Political sovereignty may thus be con- joined between the two (or more) equal entities, under some kind of Senior Constitution. That alone will take a few generations and some guts. In the past, the only way to accomplish this enlargement of union was through military conquest.... war... of one nation over another. (There was one failed attempt at this union without war in the 1950s by Gamal Nasser in Egypt and his temporary union with Syria.)

The age-old idea of full sovereignty for any country to do anything they wish will be difficult to overcome. In which book is it written that God has granted unlimited 'sovereignty' over any particular piece of land to anyone just because they happened to live there or get there first? It is the first prescription for war. There must be a better way for humans to share the resources of their world as well as the responsibility for preserving them.

Since the trend has been established toward 'participative' (laws by political initiative) rather than 'representative' democracy, a system of direct election of all members of Congress, by the voters of every member state, that is supported by appropriate political information technology, must be developed and enacted into law. There has been some limited development in this direction in the voter registration/friendship-connection systems currently in use by American political parties.

The synergistic combination of the first three North American states... Canada, Mexico and the United States,..... all of which have strong democratic traditions and are oriented toward peace, would have the political,

economic and military strength to act as a magnet
for voluntary combination with other countries. The
incentives required for the peoples of two (or more)
nations to voluntarily merge their societies are difficult
to imagine. Even overcoming modest prejudices or social
differences as groups intermix across former boundaries
can be overwhelming.

We can remember the conflicts and emotions of
the joining of the original 13 English colonies in North
America... whose lands were contiguous and people were
of the same background and spoke the same language...
and were pushed-together by a war with a common
enemy. But the time has come for us to further consider
the matter. We may have no choice, if we wish to avoid
another war. Sovereign countries tend to breed their own
kings and dictators who then want wars to get themselves
more power.

We are seeking some kind of logical nucleus to form
a world government that is stronger than a gentlemen's
club (the UN... the EU?). Change the UN? Seriously?
Its General Assembly is a classically disastrous 'pure
democracy'...an impossibly weak cacophony of equal
states, each with one vote, lead by a Security Council that
can be blocked five different ways by the veto power.
Change the European Union? After which civil war?

Considering a future North American Union, can
you realistically think of any other such combination of
states that could develop the necessary power to attract
other unions? Remember the nearly constant warfare of
Rome to maintain its vassal states? Observe the frivolous
(and even senseless) fracturing of good political unions in
the name of 'sovereignty' (Slovakia, Scotland, Pakistan)?
The smaller and weaker states that are the result of
this 'Balkanization' often predict future instability and
wars. New ideas and details on representation of these
disparate sections of the world must be developed and

documented. Over a period of many generations, peaceful expansion of the political system to encompass every present country, region and ethnic group in the world must be envisioned. Such expansion would, of course, be started by a request of some country to become a member of the new union. Such a request would only be made, or accepted, if the union would equally benefit all parties. Again, impossible? The many economic agreements now binding different world regions, such as the World Trade Organization, are a beginning of this process.

Laws and policies covering the establishment and political control of extra-terrestrial colonies must be enacted. They are coming. Remember the American Revolutionary War, which fractured a British Empire that could not imagine colonials desiring independence? Unimagined material wealth may come to our planet from mineral-rich asteroids…. if we can learn how to share. (You cannot really believe the fractious United Nations could get this done.)

The Present US Constitution: Article 2

The Executive: to build a stronger **Executive**… a triumvirate Office of the President, instead of one overwhelmed person… and select the three persons from an experienced group of tested leaders. Provision must be also enacted by an amendment for a senior elected Council of regional leaders from which experienced presidents may be drawn. No more populist opportunists or magicians or Caesars. This Senior Council of elected leaders from different world regions would eventually form the primary leadership… working with a slightly more powerful Office of the President…(remember 'Checks and Balances')…. of a slowly uniting world. And it is clear that world leadership for the forseeable future…. a majority of the Senior Council and two of the three Presidents…. will come from North America…

for the initial period of development. We will discuss reasons for this... and planned modifications in later chapters. Of course, under a Senior Constitution there would be a provision for planned self-modification to permit world leadership by any region of the world that met such established criteria for that leadership, with such leadership modification permitted very slowly.... say every fifty or one-hundred years. Remember: "Tie the hands of the majority with the bonds of a difficult to change Constitution to protect the rights of minorities."

The Present US Constitution: Article 3

The Judiciary must be carefully strengthened to retain present checks and balances in the new political system, without dominating. The present trend of "packing" the Supreme Court by Presidents who wish to control the laws must be limited. Thoughtless Presidents who do this are weakening the entire Constitutional system for their narrow interests.

The present American Constitution has just 7 Articles. Beautiful simplicity. The essence of power. Compare this to the laws with thousands of pages now produced to befuddle us all.

The Present US Constitution: Amendments

Lists of fundamental laws and rights that apply to all people, and methods of effecting changes to those laws. As present, amendments must be continually possible, but slow and difficult. Our combined wisdom is not adequate for us to make quick changes. There are too many things that stimulate our mass passions. We must be forced to wait, and prepare for change.

There is another factor that must infiltrate the consideration of all the following systems of civilization... **that of cyclical change in the feelings of all the people** who will be influenced by and who will ultimately control the events which we will attempt to influence. This is particularly important in political systems. We see this cyclical change in the American political system with the 'critical re-alignment' of the voters in the years 1860 (Lincoln), 1932 (Roosevelt) and 1980 (Reagan). This historical political movement between greater centralization of power and greater distribution of power was a source of conflict for hundreds of years in ancient Greece (600–400 BC), the Roman Republic (509–27 BC) and also in the English Civil War period (1640–60 AD). Did they ever get it right? Remember Shay's rebellion in Massachusetts? The American Civil War?

Constitutions are by definition inflexible…. unchanging lists of laws on which to base a stable government and social system. Perhaps a better constitution would allow certain laws to bend slowly in anticipation (not as a result) of peoples demands for more freedom and their opposite cries for stronger leadership. In times of peace and plenty, people demand less government…. more freedom and independence. As war or disaster approaches people lose self-confidence and seek protection in stronger government. We must accept the frivolity of mankind, and use this knowledge. This probably cannot be done without a system whereby certain laws are modified based on some kind of a predictive computer model. These concern the power of a president/chief-administrator versus the power of the congress of lawmakers.

We Need Not Look Far…

We need not look far to discover the places in the world where government is best. These are the destinations of the world's migrants who want to improve their lives: United States, Canada, Australia, New Zealand, the UK, and much of western Europe.

Yes, there are good governments elsewhere, but one must search carefully.

A good governmental system efficiently serves all people who relate to it. It serves the needs of individuals by giving them a voice in the laws that rule them and by providing support for each in difficult times... and in staying out of their way in good times. The quality of the voice of the people and the quality of the support provided depends on resources available and the dedication of the people who provide services.

In addition, the system should provide information for those who must make laws and those who must govern.

Ideally, laws should provide clear guidelines for peoples' activities, and they should treat all people the same. In fact, in much of the world in the year 2014, complex thickets of laws have been put in place to benefit only a few. These laws are made by legislators who have been specially rewarded to service a select few. the result of this type of corruption is an arcane nest of laws that are understandable to only a few who are trained in the law.

After thousands of years of experience, it should be possible for legislatures to identify and write only those laws necessary for the effective functioning of the related governmental bodies... and to get rid of the rest. But they do not get any extra 'rewards' for that... and they do not care about how simple and clear laws that make no exceptions would benefit their people. The design of any improved political system should begin with the re-writing of laws to eliminate corruption. Such laws cannot be improved by the civil servants who administer the laws, because they would be reducing the need for their own services. Only a dedicated and strong elected

President, Governors and other leaders may be motivated to do this.

Reducing the number and complexity of laws would reduce the amount of work legislators must do and reduce the overall cost of government. A simpler legal system would ultimately reduce the number of lawyers and political lobbyists who live off the system. An effort to do this would be as difficult as reducing the power of unionized civil servants.

A simpler set of laws would permit an information system that could monitor and administer the laws, making the work of legislators easier.

Legislators with less paper work to do could spend more time serving voters and improving the quality of life of their constituents. This should be the true goal of a utopian political system.

The Heart of an Improved Political System Would Be the Voter Information System (VIS)

Groups working with President Obama in recent elections have begun work on a primitive information system that identifies relationships between different voters in order to influence their votes. Is this some stupid attempt to implement a one-party dictatorship in the United States? There are also computer systems used to keep track of laws as they move through the political process. And, of course, there are many different budgetary, expense accounting and other computerized governmental financial systems. We can do more. The design of such a computerized legislative information system would be based on some of the following criteria:

> **The purpose of government is to provide for the security of the people, structure for the economic system, leadership and public services. improved government planning will improve services**

which in turn will make the economy better and increase employment. the object of an improved governmental system will be to prevent war through effective government action. is this a new concept?

There are many signs of poor government: they generally relate to poor government services, roads that fall apart, bridges that collapse, buildings that collapse, kids that are homeless and sick, people who are forgotten, people who are angry and rebellious. Consistent with the overall economy, good government should provide basic services to all people: passable roads, trains and ferries that do not kill.

a) We seek therefore to design a government and political system what will optimally meet the needs of all people within the overall economic system. The government will function as a result of the political system. The political system will function with information provided by a Voter Information System.

b) The structure of the proposed political system would be worldwide and would be designed to provide more personal contact between voters and their leaders. It would grow slowly in scope as more countries joined the world system. Its design would have to plan for and accommodate to the growth. Here we design from the completed worldwide system backwards to existing regions and countries, using the BUI concept.

In a representative democratic government, as projected for the entire world, about 2,000 representatives (1 male and 1 female) would be elected by all registered voters in about 1,000 election districts throughout the world. With an estimated three (3) billion worldwide voters (out of 4 billion population.... yes, there are about 7 billions in 2014), each representative to the lower house of the World Congress would represent about 1.5 million constituents... more than double the existing ratio (about 1 to 600k) in the United States. To improve communication, each representative would control a cadre of about 250 trained full-time persons, called 'Escorts', each of whom would maintain contact with and provide assistance to about 6000 voters. (The old 'span of control' management ideas have been greatly changed by the advent of modern information systems.)

The computerized Voter Information System would provide each Representative with full knowledge of the policies and actions of the Executive branch, the ideas and activities of all other legislators and the background and history of all existing laws and those proposed, including analysis of how existing and past laws have related to the Constitution... and the cultural impact of those laws. It would bridge the gap between the Representatives and their group of Escorts and Escort Managers by providing continual real-time detailed control and exception reports on all Escort activities. The Voter Information System would also provide each Escort with summary and detail data on laws proposed by and other activities of the related Representative and other Representatives., as well as data concerning the needs and desires of the voters served by each Escort.

Each Escort would contact electronically or in person 20 to 30 voters each work day, so that each voter would have some contact and assistance from the political system representative once or twice per year. Special need reports would be provided each Escort, with summaries for the Representative and Escort managers, so that each voter with special problems or demands would not feel neglected. It is estimated that this increased contact will result in more satisfied voters and a more stable political system.

c) The computerized system would monitor and record all contacts between all public officials and all other persons. This would control special rewards being given to legislators to propose laws to benefit only a few at the expense of the many. Contacts outside of the recorded system would be felony offenses. No more secret deals made in rest-rooms at cocktail parties. Non-public (prohibited) legislative activities and data would be recorded, rejected and reported by the 'system'.

d) The computer system would be closely audited on a continuing basis by technical experts (including a group of well-rewarded and managed genius teenage hackers) trained to detect illegal activity or tampering with the computer systems.

e) The computer system would support the work of each legislator in every way…. providing rapid and accurate information on proposed laws, laws in place, potential Constitutional conflicts, statistical analyses of the results of laws passed, lists of constituents in need of assistance, summaries of the activities of legal assistants and of groups and individual Escorts on their staff, control of messages from Escorts and constituents, projects assigned to Escorts and assistants, expenses and costs of all actual and future projects, time scheduling for public appearances including names of contacts with histories and family trees of contacts and needy constituents. The list of potential services provided by the Voter Information System is unlimited… subject only to the creative imagination of the elected official and his/ her group of Escorts… and to the types of information files made available to the system…. always under the watchful eye of the omnipresent auditors… who are also carefully managed.

Conceptually, the computerized Voter Information System is designed to improve the legislative function by allowing an elected congress-person more time alone to consider laws by giving each more control over constituent access. Their computer consoles in home and office (or tiny machines similar to the I-pod that are worn or embedded) permit them to conference-call or electronically visit with all people who they wish to see… be it other congress- persons, assistants, wealthy donors, persons asking for help, Escorts and/or Escort managers, persons asking for legislation or legal information, et cetera…. with automatic monitoring and recording of all conversations, rapid background checking of people asking favors, and warning of illegal activities.

It also enables the elected Congress-person to effectively service many more constituents through a large group of trained Escorts who can filter demands on the Congress-person's time. While the Congress-person can do more thinking, even though they are serving more than a million constituents, the Escorts can do much of their personal contact work… the Voter Information System allowing the Congressperson to control the work of hundreds of Escorts with summary reports on the work of all Escorts and detailed reports of work done by each Escort, clients contacted, suggestions from voters and problems solved for constituents in the field. The Voter Information System spans the greater gap between Congressperson and constituent by having the Escorts look out for the needs of individual voters on a much more personal basis… the Escorts having the computer equipment available to communicate easily with the few thousand constituents that are their responsibility. Greater services to the voters should result in more satisfied voters… and a more stable political system. As a negative point, it could also make voters more dependent on government.

f) Costs and other details of the proposed Voter Information System and the Escort system cannot be estimated at this time, but it is expected that the overall expense of the future political system will be much less than that of the present worldwide system. There will be less legal work to do, and it will be done more efficiently, and the costs will be spread over the entire world system. And the new system will be designed to control the present corruption.

Lane 4: The Education System
Education is discussed more fully in Chapter 8.

As the world changes during the next centuries, education must also change. While vocational training may dominate schools of the 21st Century, the more distant future will have a completely different career matrix, and education may focus on science, communication, social interaction, emotional and physical pleasure, hobbies, creative crafts and the arts.

Government must establish and maintain educational standards and institutions to teach children and persons of other age levels facts, skills, values and attitudes that will prepare them for employment, parenthood and all other activities in the world culture. Student motivation and self- discipline will remain a challenge to educators.

Primary education of children in the 22rd Century will be mostly course-lozenge, telepathy-put or computerized except for physical education, recreational sports and nature-enjoyment training, which will require many teachers.

Since teens are more involved with peer acceptance and often rebel against parental influence, school after age 13 should be centralized, with live-in students (increasing and controlling peer influence and reducing parental conflicts). This is in-fact practiced in many cultures in the 21st Century.

Secondary education should cover math and language/communication skills, history, science, world economic geography, cultural anthropology, leadership, art appreciation, health, entrepreneurship, bookkeeping, cosmology and physical development. Job skills taught in the last two secondary years must relate to available jobs. Teacher pay must equal that of other skilled professions, and must involve qualitative monitoring... as in other professions. Teachers and students must be evaluated annually and held to universal standards.

Ways may be found to directly induce learning into the brain (human and other animal) using programmed-bio-chemical processes (first, expensive injections... later, suppositories and lozenges, or skin-implants) and/ or tiny ultra-powerful I-pod-like devices implanted or otherwise interacting with the brain.... which will greatly change education. These 'advances' will require close governmental control to avoid related social disasters. At first, only the rich will be able to afford these 'tutorial' devices.

The immense power of small hand-held computing and communications devices will be put to use in education ... in addition to satisfying the social needs of students. This will require improved educational research.

Lane 5: Economics

This is a difficult area, which we can only touch on here. We need time to explore the myriad options. And we need the help of experts, although it is a big risk to trust any present authority too much. The Socialists, communists, capitalists and whatever are still locked in gentle academic combat in many universities, with few faculty able to rise above the fray. Eventually they will reach some accommodation. However, we can look into the future to examine some possibilities.

Assuming that the world economic system can be changed to be less subject to corruption and collapse, perhaps by again converting to a gold standard, with fewer separate countries there will be less international finance. And then what happens when we discover an asteroid of nearly solid gold, silver or platinum... like the discovery of the silver Comstock Lode in Nevada during the American Civil War? We have no idea of what riches may lie ahead in space. But we need to plan for the possibility.

Cities and urban complexes will dominate private business. Perhaps money will be eliminated and replaced by a credit system that will guarantee all persons with a living income regardless of profession, ambition or location. People who do not wish to work may not need to work at all. Will that make them happy?

Most jobs will be in human services. Departments of Education will be more important. Military services will be smaller and highly specialized for monitoring a peaceful society and a possibly fractious group of planetary colonies.

Many different 'counselors' are suggested in education and society to assist people in finding happiness in their lives. We will have to discover whether this is appropriate, and how to pay for all those counselors. And who will worry about all those counselors being happy? It is too early to determine exactly how an on-going economic system will balance the costs of various changes with savings from other changes. They may be expensive, but so are wars … and the preparation for wars.

After several centuries of preparation, the most perfect world will be one of stability. No wars. No famine or pestilence. Few manufacturing jobs… robots will do almost all heavy work. Boring? Happy? It depends on your viewpoint.

If we do not destroy cities in wars, we will not have to re-build them, saving a lot of expense. If we have a stable population that is living where they wish to live, aside from a few congenital wanderers, why will they wish to move? On earth, we can foresee jobs in human services, sciences and the arts. There always will be need for government workers, teachers, entertainers, counselors, trainers, managers, medical persons, sex therapists and helping persons. There will be small service-oriented businesses. Government may control terrestrial and space travel, but large corporations with investment capital may develop colonies on the planets and asteroids. Scientists will still be needed to probe the unknown... the regions will still be vast. Artists and creative persons will reach for new beauty... to great acclaim. And there will be the new professions and work opportunities.

On earth after the 22nd Century, there may be no need for money. In a stable population, with stable needs, perhaps conspicuous consumption will be passé. In the best possible world, everyone will have the home they wish and it will not depend on income. Perhaps all work-related incomes will be regulated... depending on education, effort, benefits to society and need. Work may depend on motivation... with jobs awarded to only part of the people. Are we backing into a world of socialism? We do not seek that. We need to keep a balance.

In the name of stability, family size may be limited, therefore standardizing the need for educational and training facilities. Manufacturing and farming will be stable and limited to need... and most work will be done by robots. People who wish to become rich and seek challenge may be forced to emigrate to the other planets or the many asteroids. New forms of government will be needed for these entities. The new frontiers will be limitless.

6

POSSIBLE SCIENTIFIC INNOVATIONS

Possibly, by the year 2210, we will have become suspicious of all innovation. Science has brought us from the dark ages (about 500–1200 AD) to the wonders or curses of atomic power, computers, robots, and prolonged life. The flooding and warming problems of the 21st Century may be solved by the 22nd Century through the use of huge solar reflectors in space to modify the cloud cover… heating or cooling the earth as we need…. Reducing night or cold winters if we wish.

New technical hardware will be designed and built by robots. Micro-electronic technology will continue as an important area of engineering. Macro-engineering will produce huge machines, such as those necessary to build giant sea walls, underground cities and to hollow-out a moon.

New methods of transportation may bring greater mobility to people and distant products to their tables. Disease and sickness may have been eliminated… changing the health-care industries everywhere…. and leaving us vulnerable to unknown diseases…. and with a population of geriatrics. Life spans will have increased greatly through genetic manipulation and organ transplant…. for those who can afford it.

Governmental policies, investment and controls may be needed in the areas of scientific inquiry. The following ideas are the result of simple linear projection of present-day innovation combined with a recognition of need:

Languages

A revolution in language use and translation will begin in less than a decade. Hand-held electronic devices are approaching the power and sophistication to accomplish high-speed colloquial translation that will permit people to speak into the device and instantly words, phrases and full sentences of another language will be projected to a listener (while being recorded and transmitted, if desired). Eventually, the devices will be small enough to be emplantable in the throat and will be able to generate more than one language at once, switchable by thought. Thought transmission and feelings transmission simultaneous with speech will follow less than a generation later.

A world divided by language will end. One cause for war will also end.

Boring: Continued development of present-day boring machines (now able to cut tunnels more than 15 feet ... 5 meters... wide), combined with ever-higher fuel costs that will eventually reduce air travel,will see great expansion in long-distance near-speed-of-sound rail travel on magnetically-levitated trains. One potential project, a high- speed rail line between Seattle (USA) and Beijing (China) at near sea level cutting through mountains and under the Bearing Strait that separates Alaska from Russia. When the boring machines are fully automated and heat insulated, a straight-line tunnel from the two sides of the 80-mile channel (instead of a curved tunnel that follows the earth's curvature below the floor of the sea) will approach a depth of about 4 miles and encounter constant heat from the rocks that will permit a new kind of earth-powered electrical generation that may be adequate to power all trains at above 600 mph between the two cities. The trains would connect the two cities in less time than present airliners, with lower cost and greater safety.

With continued development of gigantic boring machines, temperature-controlled underground cities and even farmland on earth, the moon and other planets may be envisioned.

Collisions: By the 22nd Century laser telescope technology may have scanned the universe out to ten light years to detect and eventually destroy any asteroid that is large enough to threaten the earth. By the 23rd Century this protection may have extended out to 100 light years.

With glaciers possibly coming, an effort may be underway to increase carbon-dioxide levels in the stratosphere in order to increase global warming. If glacial ages are caused by variations in the oblong orbit of the earth around the sun, this orbit of the earth may be modified by a series of huge rocket motors located in series around the earth parallel to the actual movement of the earth (approximately at the equator). By firing these rockets sequentially at the moment the rotation of the earth brings them in direct opposition to the earth's movement around the sun, the orbit of the earth may be modified enough to prevent the glacial period... but not enough to destroy the earth by moving it too close to the sun.

Space-nets: The thousand-square-kilometer solar collectors used to generate electricity in the 22nd Century may be maneuvered to catch the low-speed solar wind energy, with laser-cabling to the earth stations, to reduce the elliptical solar orbit (and related cooling) of the earth.

The Kaiser-Needles:

Following the development of new *stronger and lighter metals,* inter-planetary commerce may be made practical on heavy-atmosphere/strong gravity planets (such as Earth) by the construction of slim towers that reach up above the atmosphere (about 15 km at the poles) to provide docking/launch platforms for space-transporters. This will allow light-weight rockets (less heat-shielding, smaller engines, less fuel) to shuttle between earth and moon (the real future space-travel center), transporting out-migrating humans and incoming manufactures. These vertical needles will have to be placed near the north and south poles to reduce the static electricity effect of the spinning earth on the towers (zero mph at the two poles, about 100 mph at northern Greenland (about 81 degrees north latitude) and about 1000 mph at the equator). Northern Greenland or Baffin Island locations would benefit from ice-free summer shipping of heavy equipment and may also be connected to temperate-zone industrial resources via high-speed magnetic-rail lines bored directly north from Quebec through the rocks and permafrost of northern Canada.

Since workmen cannot build at great heights, the towers may have to be raised into the sky with robots, one 100 foot-long segment at a time (similar to how oil wells are drilled down into the earth). New four-person elevator capsules will transport humans up and down the narrow shaft with some discomfort. Other pipes will deliver fuels to the space craft. Down tubes will deliver incoming metals and items manufactured on the Moon and elsewhere. Moon transporters will coast into docking position from the west without ever having to enter the dense earth atmosphere and only slowing down to connect with the Kaiser-needle (the top of which will be moving at a bit more than 100 mph to the east).

When loaded with people headed for the moon or planets they will disconnect and leave with much less fuel use than if they were to blast off from earth surface. The transporter mass will be much less, since little heat-shielding will be needed.

Tower design cross-sections will require much experimentation to limit weather disturbances and noise caused by the shaft and support cables moving by the earth's rotation through the lower atmosphere at a constant sub-sonic speed. Huge amounts of electricity will be generated by the tower(s).

Estimating to provide the beginning of engineering design, a 6 foot (or 2 meter) diameter tower consisting of special steel that varies from perhaps 50 millimeters (2") thick at the base to 12 millimeters (.5") thick at the fifteen kilometer (50,000 ft.) top might weigh about 26,000 tons and consist of about 500 two-part segments that are about 33 meters (100 ft.) long. Each 33 meter segment would be divided in half down the length of the tube, and each piece would weigh an average of about 13 tons. Guessing a cost of about $200k for each piece, or a total of about $100 million, for a total project cost estimate at perhaps $300 million. At a saving of perhaps $10 million for each rocket that would not be needed to blast off from sea-level, the tower may pay for itself in 3 years by eliminating the need for ten sea-level rocket launches per year.

Lifted into place at the tower base, with rails welded at the sides of the half-tube and two gear-strips welded at 1/3 the half-diameter, robot control of internal cog motors would raise each segment-half up the outside of the tower until reaching the last segment at the top. At this point, a robot controlled shaft inside the existing tube would attach itself to the top of the two new half-segments and, using robot controlled cog-motors on the interior of the tube, lift the two half-segments until they seat themselves against flanges on the top edge of each segment. Then robot welding devices may weld the new segments together and to the top of the previous two segments. Testing will determine the actual type and thickness of the steel needed. Special stretch-resisting steel guy wires spreading out in four directions every 100 meters will hold the tower in place.

Even at the relatively slow-speed location on Baffin Island the tower and guy wires will generate huge amounts of electricity, which will power the underground town that will be located at the site. Of course this first design effort will be improved by qualified engineers and with the use of new materials that may come available by 2050, when the first tower may be needed.

Pipes and elevators inside the tower tube will transport cargo and fuel to and from space craft that would cruise in at low speed and dock at the top of the tower. Ships from the moon would need very little fuel to make the journey to the earth tower, since the two bodies are moving at near- similar speeds, and the moon has minimal gravity. Ships going to Mars would need to accelerate from the 67,000 mph speed that the earth is moving around the sun to match the speed Mars is moving around the Sun.

The heavy atmosphere of the earth will prevent it from being a manufacturing center for the planets. The moon and asteroids will do that job, along with such moons as Jupiter's Io.

Moon-junk: The moon will, or course, be the major transportation and manufacturing center, since there is no atmosphere and minimal gravity to limit take-off and landing of transporters. Retired persons may flock to the Moon for its healthy low gravity and great views of earth and heavens. Surface residential towers on the moon will house residential apartments and all offices, medical services and shopping facilities. Small (300 ft.) domes on moon-surface will provide pleasant ponds and forested parks for tower residents. Manufacturing facilities and farms may be located in 600 ft. wide caverns bored near the moon surface by huge tunneling machines possibly manufactured beginning in 2035 by Lockheed. If oxygen and hydrogen can be located in moon rocks, solar power will be able to create water from those rocks. Atomic reactors will also be relatively safe to use for power on the Moon. Any pollutants from industry on the Moon can be trapped in the zero-atmosphere environment, encapsulated, and used for building materials.

Information Systems and Communication:

The area of Information Technology and related systems may cease to exist as an area of study and development by the 22nd Century. New fields of technology will provide new directions.

Telepathic communication in the realm of human to human, human to animal and human to robot will be an accepted science. And that is just the beginning.

Spoken language will probably be in English, since it is now the only international language. Chinese, Spanish, and Russian, while spoken by hundreds of millions, are regional languages which could only be imposed worldwide as a result of wars. Hundreds of years of forced English in India, forced Spanish in Peru, and imposed German in Bohemia have not succeeded in replacing the local dialects. People's unbreakable pride in their language cannot be denied. English is important, but not ubiquitous. And it is unnecessarily complex.

If we are to seek a peaceful world community, we must consider a world language. It is possible that future computers will be powerful and small enough to permit instant translation between many languages... given that true translation is really possible (and mis-understandings are not important). And it is possible that language education may be improved enough to really improve the international use of language translation. But these answers of today do not really address the problem. And, do not talk about Esperanto.... it is a toy of academia that is far too complex and minimally used.

What we need is a language that is designed at several levels...

1. a quick-and-dirty level that will allow basic tourist and commercial communication for unchanging speakers of other languages (such as 'Pidgin').
2. an educator 's level, for those who need adequate (but not complete) fluency and understandability in their speech and writing.
3. a literary level, for writers and professional communicators.

All levels may be designed to embody common words and phrases from many international languages, in order to give all major ethnic groups the feeling that their 'mother tongue' is not being totally lost. And those dialects may be supported locally and in private schools as home languages.

Much more can be done. If an English base is truly the preferred language, those whose culture is English can say, 'We won, because we are best.' This thinking is the cause of wars, and it is stupid. It is the reason why cultural hatred has been a curse among humans for all of history. It is time we change. No culture should be allowed to 'win'.

The culture with the least necessary change in the language must be expected to pay most of the expense for the language re-design and re-education for the rest of the world. English speakers should be prepared to see major modifications to their language to make it simpler in grammar, more logical in structure and easier to learn for others. Changes in pronunciation must be expected. They should welcome major blocks of words and phrases from other cultures. This should be a major research effort.

They should pay for the development of a simplified Pidgin that is truly easy to learn and then pay for professional development of learning media and for tens of millions of low-cost copies of that media and instructor training to promulgate the new language media.

The Chinese, Japanese and Koreans will see their language changed the most, since it is not alphabet-based (except for Pinyin Chinese). Therefore they should pay the least and expect the most assistance from other cultures of the world.

And, since language differences are major causes for war, all cultures should celebrate the elimination of this cause. But, it will take generations and cost a very great amount.

Extra-Sensory Communication:

After some generations, the ability for humans to send and receive communications that consist of brain-transmitted images should enable the development of an icon language that may enhance the range of meaning of written language.... but not replace it. The icons may be standardized as full-meaning images that are not ideograms. Such images may permit two-way communication with non-human subjects with more meaning than body-language (such as smiling or tail- wagging).

Other innovation:

New entertainment devices may involve all body senses, with extra-cost fantasy and imagination extensions and variable third-party and/or group involvement.

World Systems:

The world of the distant future will be politically organized under one representative government. There will be no countries or national political boundaries, except possibly those districts where resistant radical Islam is still the state religion. Individuals or groups of people may move across the world at will. There will be no language barriers, since a modified form of English and telepathy will be taught from the age of four until 13 in all schools. Regional or ethnic languages may persist in the home where desired.

Genius, flexibility, education and luck will be required to design a planetary colonial political and economic system that will avoid the problems that gave us the American colonial revolution in 1775. It would be a pity to see a 'tea party' on Mars destroying good tea from earth that is too highly taxed.

Balancing....And Everything Else:

Or should we simply call it Wisdom? We do not know when we are being wise. We only know when we have not been wise. And then it is usually too late.

In a universal cultural system that we call civilization, nothing can be left out. Everything else… the details we have neglected or forgotten… is really everything. In our search for The Castle, we can forget neither the sparkling towers nor the rats in the foundation. Given time, the termites in the rafters can bring the entire structure down. And this system must last a long time… at least until we can find a better one.

So we must build a program to balance the entire system with innovative pieces here and there. And we must know when to stop. A big job for some very mature, wise, protected and dedicated people…. persons with the stature and respect that is reminiscent of the US Supreme Court, who employ a very bright multinational team of technical innovators.

Nationalism or inflexible religious dogma will quickly destroy any effort to build a universal cultural system.

While religious ethics and morality should be at the heart of the design effort, bending the systems to fit any existing religion or blind righteous dogma cannot be permitted.

For each person according to their desires: good health and long life, family love, adequate food and finances ... and the time to enjoy them. Do we call that utopia? The Castle?

7

POSSIBLE SCENARIOS

Here we show the results of traditional planning. Of the three traditional planning models already presented (Disruption, Cycular and Linear Progression), the most probable is:

1. The continuation of the present Cyclical trend toward Empire Amerika.

2. Obvious comparisons may be made with the empires of Hitler, Czarist and Communist Russia, Britain, Napoleon and Rome... all of which rose and fell in a cycle. The worldwide empire that is slowly taking shape under the sometime leadership of the United States has the power and momentum provided by the endless wealth of the world's great corporations and the muscle provided by the American/German/English military-industrial complex. If during the next 30 years some group like the Bilderburgers or some strong American President can formulate some kind of control structure and if the United States chooses to formally assume a leadership role, this amorphous empire may last until financial greed among its leaders collapses its financial core, causing political collapse and civil war, a cyclical repetition of the Roman collapse. Or, because it is not planned, it could become captive of some

person or small group leading to a repetition of the Napoleonic or Third Reich model. A total world collapse is possible with this module, with uncontrolled atomic weapons available to all parties. It is an unstable model that benefits the rich and has little interest in human welfare. There is at present no visible effort to control this monster, or even to recognize it.

3. Somewhat better planned is the continuing growth by the Linear Progression model of the worldwide Muslim political-religious Caliphate (kingdom). The 50% growth in population of this middle-eastern system (to more than 1.5 billion persons) is based not on the conquest of more land, but on high internal reproduction rates among existing populations in the many poverty-stricken lands it now dominates. Its growth has been based on mid-eastern oil wealth. Excessive population growth without equal economic growth has now caused great instability throughout the middle east.

4. It may use immigration and high reproduction to eventually attain political prominence in many European nations, and may soon dominate most of Europe, south Asia, much of Africa and possibly some of South America. The design of its political system is a world kingdom, based on its unchanging 6th- Century origins in Arabia. Its leadership structure is divided about 80/20 based on disagreements between Sunni and Shia factions concerning its origins. At present there is hostility between the groups and little movement toward unity. It can be expected that if the Shia state of Iran obtains the atom bomb there will be a change in the internal balance of power, with probable internal conflict. Nevertheless, this

political-religious empire with split leadership does have world-conquest ambitions.

5. The growth of a monolithic China into a dominant world hegemon, another Cyclical model of empire, is possible but doubtful. The Chinese political system is now focused on internal growth, and on an attempt to control its huge population as it is being pushed toward greater liberalism. There is little focus or tradition toward foreign expansion, and its present one-party political structure will face huge problems in coping with greater democracy. There is some chance that it will fracture in coming years, with resultant chaos. There is also the chance of some northward population movement in an attempt to find room for its excess millions.

6. The last 'Disruption-Model' catastrophes for the world was the Great Plague of the year 1347 and the worldwide devastation of World War II. While great natural disasters do occur with disturbing regularity in different parts of the world, nothing has come close to the nearly 50% loss in human life suffered by Europe and the mid-east from that Bubonic plague disaster which continued at different levels for centuries and greatly influenced the populations and histories of the affected nations. Recent earthquakes, tsunamis and typhoons have caused damage and loss of life that could have been averted by better planning and preparation... which should be a part of any improved civilization. There are controls now in place relating to world-threatening diseases. The expected world-wide disaster relating to uncontrolled global warming and the related green-house effect could approach a disaster of the Disruption Model magnitude. We choose to ignore

the expected wars of the future for the time being. Our objective is to avoid them.

Having completed a brief analysis of disasters of the future, and recognizing that it is going to take some luck for humanity to come through the next difficult years, we are ready to look at a different method of planning.

Our method is to temporarily ignore (or jump over) the horrors of the present and near future and focus on a world that is what it should be and can be, a utopia. Then, using the BUI method, we back up from that future utopia to the present to provide a 'bridge' out of the present mess.

8

THE DECADE OF 2180-90, 170 YEARS INTO THE FUTURE

(Note: this attempt is similar to asking Emperor Napoleon... in 1810... to make a plan that would envision today... 2014. If he had done so, would we still have the chaos we see today... or would it be worse? We know he did try. His legal system... Code Napoleon... is still in use today in many countries, such as Mexico.)

Is This The Castle?

No, no… this is not **'The Plan'**. This is the beginning of the First planning step. It is time to try to visualize The Castle. The Plan will reveal itself in the next chapters, as we attempt the backward iteration (BUI) process... but even then it will need much more work. A practical plan will require the ideas of many people over many years. In this BUI method, the first step is a description of the end… the Goal… The Castle in the Sky …..

A utopia is institutionalized personal satisfaction..... happiness. Aristotle again: life, liberty and the pursuit of happiness. The reason the United States was born. Did we forget? So, how do you reach for happiness for each of six billion people? How can you even define happiness on such a scale? Perhaps it is simply the freedom to be left-alone. Is that possible in a big modern city?

The beginning of civilization is farming. Just considering a rural setting for a moment, there would have to be a supportive Garden of Eden for each person .... lots of goodies to eat, nothing around with big teeth or a bigger club. Happiness for a head-hunter is getting heads.... not so happy for the original possessor. Happiness for the criminal is crime. Or is it? No poor? Or, at least no hungry, homeless and sick poor. Happy poor? No envy? No crime? Can't have the rich flaunting their wealth. No greed. But does that mean no ambition, no progress? No motivation to learn, to build? No fun?

So we must accept Aristotle's definition of happiness in terms of freedom for people to be happy in their own way, as long as that does not detract from the happiness or freedom of others. This requires a set of behavior codes, or laws, that all people accept. Can one set of laws be designed for the whole world? Yes, as long as they follow generally accepted behavioral patterns. And, we will need education to teach the rules and a political system to enforce the rules and provide security and other services, such as counseling in obeying rules. And it requires an accepted moral code that gives the laws validity. Is there a moral code that fits for peoples in Mongolia and Costa Rica? There are family and other cultural differences, but the basic values are very similar. Once we can document and understand most of the similarities and differences of most of the world's cultures we can move on. From there we can progress rapidly to the Social, Moral, Political, and Educational systems discussed below.... with the basic understanding that all these interrelated parts of a civilization are herein focused on utopian goals... human happiness and no war.... That will take a while to figure out.

And then we must consider the most challenging aspect of all.... the spiritual. Can a civilization exist without the spiritual? And, where do we begin that study?

But, most important… a utopia will have to be without motivation for war or mass murder. And that means no political borders to fight over and no hostile religious groups. Or no religious groups at all? One world, with robust controls on group hatred. Just how do you do all that? Do we leave that to a king or a dictator to tell us how?

Due to personal magnetism or spiritual commitment, some persons who choose to be shamans or other religious leaders can bring joy to some and trouble to society. Those who choose to be religious leaders must also accept responsibility to the government for their words and actions to be within the limits of the law. However, there will still probably be isolated religious groups that refuse to integrate with the rest of the world society (unless they can be boss). They can be left in peace in their own areas and with their own ideas, but if they must proselytize or are any threat to their neighbors they must be kept insulated and monitored using satellites, airborne electronics and police until they choose to moderate their views.

To Begin

Keep in mind that behind all the factors discussed below lies a set of laws, a Constitution, that is modeled after the United States Constitution (with amendments and court interpretations) of the time around 2015 AD… but with certain needed improvements. We tentatively choose the Constitution of the United States of America because it is the basis for many of the constitutions in the world of 2015. It provides the political matrix around which all subsequent improvements are built.

Before proceeding too far, we should examine the constitutions of many countries, looking for improvements. This will reveal that many Constitutions follow the general pattern of that of the USA, however, some have clearly been written as confusing and obfuscatory documents to keep in power many family-controlled governments in the world.... with page after page of meaningless guarantees of absurd benefits that cannot possibly be provided by government. Also, many fail to provide strong checks and balances. Kings and dictators love weak Constitutions.

The base of any civilization is work and education. In all societies people need work in order to eat. In farming cultures people eat by working on family farms. In other cultures people need to find work that will pay for the food they must buy from farms. That requires education to learn skills needed to work and to raise children. Much home-making education can be given by parents, but skills in earning money are usually learned in some formal school. Therefore, among the primary reasons for government is schools and defense against those who would enslave the people. An economic system is nurtured by government to provide funds for schools and security against intruders. The economic system provides the basis for all work.

To Present Our Utopia: Earth-Planet Date—July 2182

Please picture in your mind the first meeting of a welcoming committee with a travel-worn group of human visitors from the earth-colony on Io, the only moon of Jupiter that is not cloaked in miles-thick ice. Io is a moon that has very many dangerous active volcanoes. The group has made the 400-million mile trip in about 50 earth-days at about 67,000 miles per hour by using the approximate 37,000 mph speed of Io around Jupiter (which moves around the sun at about 30,000 mph) to sling-shot the space craft to reach the earth and moon, which move at about 65,000 mph around the sun. Everything going to the high-gravity Earth-planet stops first at the low-gravity moon-colony to change to craft that are safe for the Earth.

The Earth-planet spokesperson speaks school-book English to the distinguished visiting group, most of whose forefathers left the earth several generations before....

Most excellent greeting!

You, ah.... Yes, here we are pleased you come... and most large welcome!

Ah, are you still tired?... We know it is hard to wake-up after you have slept for many weeks on your journey from Jupiter- moon Io. Of course, you were awake for entry. Were you upset by the 15 kilometer ride down the entry tower from your transporter dock? We know the elevator is very tight for space, and the sudden deceleration after the 6-minute zip down the needle can be uncomfortable.

I try speak to you in your Archaic-English, which I have studied when we know you will come here. I maybe got one of Archaic-English 'language-suppositories' out of sequence. I hope you understand me.

As I speak to you, I also communicate with my friends here on our 'hello' committee in Standard Icon Telepathy (we say 'St- i-T') and also with our Normal Emotion Bong. I try to use NOT our Commonspeak language of today here.

We hope maybe you wish to bring our St-i-T programs and Commonspeak Language–Lozenge learning system to Io-moon with you.

Ah..., excuse please... Jim, in hello-welcome group here, is blasting me in my head with telepathy-icons while I try to speak correct Archaic-English to you. Ah! ... makes me the dizzyness! Jim does worry I do NOT forget the each-person introduction.

I am speaking Archaic-English to you for our hello-committee, and there are happy and friendly icons bashing me in my head… and all wish to greeting-shake your hand! We send you strong Emotion-Bong very warm friendship-smile and sincere good hello!

Ah, you send to me Emotion-Bong 'TIRED'! Very sorry. To continue after you rest. Here now hand-carry e-book for you to read old-style Archaic-English more…. Thankyou OK much!

On E-Pad Hand-Held Display

Greetings to the Io Visitors Committee; New Washington, 14 July 2182

We wish your long journey and your earth-year here to benefit to all Io-moon people and also to Earth-planet Commonwealth. We wish this summary of our stable Earth-planet System to answer your many question.

The many friendship between Earth-planet and Sygmoid of Autonomous Io-moon Industrial Province is very-very to us.

Here you can read-see old Archaic-English effort to make written communication to you!! Please to overlook the stupidity mistake!

Summary: Our civilization is now a complex seven-lane interacting system, developed over many generations from first concepts outlined in the second decade of 21st Century. The seven interacting processes are:

1. Cultural
2. Environment
3. Political
4. Educational
5. Economic
6. Language
7. Religion

Other system-wide factors, such as security and war-prevention are discussed outside the main lanes of development.

Space considerations in this memo force us to include here only the Cultural and Environment Lanes.

Lane 1: Year 2180, Earth-Planet–Cultural System

On Earth-planet we now have stable education system to prepare all person to be productive in work-job that is always OK pleasant, interesting, not very demanding in effort or time, OK pay and give some flexibility in life. From child-time we learn pet-cat kindness, count-ten tolerant, tai-chee work-off anger and wide-grin hanky-panky. Job pay based on social benefits and market factors in areas homemaking, teaching/caring, counseling, government services, science development, science research, environmental improvement, farming arts, security services, transport arts, finance/large industry, small business, religious services, professional services, creative arts, sports and recreation and self-concern. All economic organizations based on market viability. Work week standard 'four by four '.... 4 hours per day 4 days per week. Retirement age variable, based on market needs and personal investment factors.

Stay on earth-planet to relax, have good life, wide-grin and happy. To take-risk and maybe rich, must to go to new solar-colony. Colonies now in large tunnels made on Earth-moon and Mars-planet and Io-moon of Jupiter, in ice on Ganymede and Europa-moons of Jupiter, and in surface domes on Venus. Mercury-planet dome colony disaster will be again attempted in future after robot dome- constructors attain better heat insulation.

Most town, city or other living center on earth-planet and colonies have low-cost fun-center facility with several swim-pool, game rooms, video libraries, electronic equipment, exercise equipment rooms, saunas, hide-and- seek warrens with wide-grin nests, social-speak pubs, bridge and marriage-partner game rooms, casino and small hot-tub single and group play rooms, astronomy center with telescopes, biological nature center, classrooms, art/sculpture labs, wood/metal workshop, vehicle repair, chem/geology lab, small auditorium-symphony hall, gymnasium and game field (all monitored for security) where persons of all ages may romp. There is no communicable disease on Earth-planet.

Young worker age 18–30 have close-counsel for early job-satisfaction, work-skill better, social acceptance, physical-attractive/sweet-smell, group outdoor-in-door wide-grin and other sport activity and self-acceptance. Re-training as necessary. Group-counsel for chase-trick, dating, match-making, dumb-stupid, social group and future job satisfaction.

Older worker counsel-help in job-progression, bossing, handling change, pay-bills, marriage and family, wide- grin and physical problem, recreation, music and art appreciation, taxes and retire/financial planning. OK-web of social support, failure-control/pick-up, personal- satisfaction counsel and family support assist for all persons.

Retirement age optional, depend on productivity in chosen field. Counsel to assist personal-utopia-search, happiness matrix, retirement fun, endless hanky-panky and life-stability.

While the potential for wide-grin now enhanced through natural selection, human genes relating to violence now hormone-reduced, eliminating passion-related crime. Social training includes full acceptance of temporary liaisons among men and women that can enrich permanent relationships. All liaisons counselor-monitored.

Lane 2: Year 2180, Earth-Planet–Environment

In time-span of only one-hundred years, we now begin to re-freeze polar ice-caps (after building polar underground mining cities deep in rock) to reduce ocean levels to year 2,000... Get new farmland/forest in Florida, Amazonia, Bangladesh, Indonesia areas.

Also move Earth-planet out of its glacier-coming orbit using many giant hydrogen-ion rockets built around equator and which fire sequentially to push against (to slow-down) Earth-planet movement around Sun-star.

With population export to now 18 space and planetary colonies, Earth-planet now has stable systems. Present four-billion Earth-planet population now in balance with food production. All eat OK good. No more eat grass or own kids.

Pollution level now reduced to age 1800s because all energy now provided by Earth-core plasma-steam-generators and by space-based power grid capturing solar energy in thousand-square-kilometer space-sails. Space- sails also used to focus solar-wind-energy where cloud- cover needed to produce new forest and farm-land in Sahara, central Asia, Australia and Mojave-desert.

Earth-plasma-power now air-condition all hot-land dome cities....bring 115-degree (Fahrenheit) outside to 75-degree comfort inside, for all work, recreation and wide-grin hanky-panky.

Climate is modified to provide forest, grassland and farmland over all possible areas of Earth-planet, including major desert areas. Most heavy industry now relocated off-planet or in self-contained caverns. Growth industries located off-planet in colonies with no Earth-tax.

City-Public transport encouraged through adequate tax on private (non-farm) vehicle and power-grid-use. Replacement manufacturing now underground or off-planet. Non-farm work-week is 4 by 4 (four hours per day, 16 hr. week). **Wage rate and benefits now keyed to regional productivity on a world-system-comparison basis.** Less wage differential means less worker migration and social disturbance.

To: Io Visitors Committee–Summary of Other Lanes

Earth-planet educational system now standardized to produce peaceful and productive world society. International boundary and language difference that in past time produce many hostility now all gone. To maintain peace, must people educated to be happy, productive and politically flexible. Now all Earth-planet has many generation of constitutional rule by law.... built from ancient U.S. Amerimexican constitution and amendments. Still here we have OK Bill of Rights freedoms. Not so much freedom now to kill and do war. Also maybe no freedom to yell-fire! or loud-fart in crowded room. All do learn rules to live and be happy.

Prior period 21st Century wars and famines, and later migration to space colonies reduce Earth-planet to 4 billion population, maintained through migration and family- planning. Family-size set by Region to maintain zero- growth population. Larger families freedom-permitted, but more taxed for extra services.

Cities destroyed or moved by war or rising ocean now relocated onto marginal lands as automated transportation tower-communities or in underground or under-ocean complexes. Other cities re-designed and reduced in size to provide green-park, private garden plot for veggie and half-hour monorail forest access to all resident. Town of smaller than 40,000 bodies receive extra government support, and residents pay lower taxes.

End of Io Visitors Committee memo. We continue below with a discussion of system Lanes that are more complex.

Lane 3: 2180, Earth-Planet–Political Systems A

On Earth-planet, now one Constitution law for all. All one government, except for insulated Sharia Reservations.

> Fully representative/participative democracy for all Earth-planet.
>
> No separate country or political unit. No reason for war. No one wants insurrection.

One controlled language Commonspeak is taught, other languages used in home only. All persons trained in Standard Icon Telepathy and in using emotional 'bongs'. Wrist-watch-size translators thought-controlled to speak 160 of most common home languages.

Political design envisions powerful central core of government for efficient decision-making with internal checks and balances of Executive Office/Senate/ Judicial and a civilian-controlled security system. Supreme political power remains in the written Global Constitution, which is supported by an Executive and a bi-cameral Legislature and guarded by a vigilant life-time-secure Supreme Court. A carefully monitored computer-based Voter Information System connects legislators to their multitude constituencies everywhere through local fully-controlled Escort (messenger) persons to provide personal-contact voter support and feedback.

Governmental functions in stable-system period are much smaller, more efficient and cost-effective than government in 21st Century. The Senate (senior house in legislature) has strong review of Executive decisions, and power of impeachment. Senate originates financial legislation, including funding of security and intelligence, and approves all laws passed by lower House of Representatives before submitting to Executive for approval/implementation. Very few new laws needed each year.

Executive and Senate and Representative core (and
families) are dispersed for security and heavily protected.
Large House of Representatives communicates with
Senate and Executive via most-secure information
system which facilitates instant conferencing and voting
from anywhere. Instant locator system facilitates rapid
decision-making.

Law-Making Is Less

Stable social-political system requires fewer and more
simple laws. Many laws re-written over time. Less work
for Congress. Government is cheaper.

Earth-planet **Executive Counsel consists** of one man
and one lady leader from each of 13 major Regions of
Earth-planet, with an additional member from each of
the three North American Regions. Office of the President
consisting of three Presidents of equal power (and one
non-voting vice-President). For the first 50 years of the
new political system, two of the Presidents and the
Vice- President were selected from North American
Regions. Now, no Region can dominate for more than 20
years. Presidents are elected from the Executive Counsel
members who have at least one year tenure by secret
ballot of all members of the **World Congress.** Each two-
years one or two new Presidents is elected for a 4 year
term to replace those sitting members of the Office of the
Presidency whose terms expire, with no President allowed
more than two four year terms. Presidents may attend
Executive Council sessions, and may vote. Each President
is assigned focus responsibilities, such as military/
colonial-matters, earth-planet cultural stability/cabinet
liaison and Earth-Congress/Judicial liaison. All deal with
on-going religious mediation/arbitration.

The Vice-President is elected by and from members
of the Earth Congress for a term of four years to coincide
with Presidential election years. He or she heads special

projects assigned by Office of Presidency and replaces incapacitated members of the Office of the Presidency until the end of their respective term. The Vice President may vote in the Office of the Presidency and the Executive Counsel only to break ties.

As a part of the system of checks and balances: A majority vote of the Executive Council can over-rule the decision of one of the Presidents. A two-thirds majority of the Executive Council can over-rule the decisions of two Presidents or initiate impeachment of one President. A three-quarter majority can initiate impeachment of two Presidents at once. Two agreeing Presidents or a majority of World Senate members may initiate impeachment of any one of the Executive Council members. Any such impeachments are to be tried in the entire World Congress, with a simple majority vote of the World Senate to convict. Impeached and convicted persons are immediately retired from office (including their seat in the World Congress, if any) with no paid staff and reduced benefits equal to that of a retired senior civil servant. Crimes and misdemeanors may be additionally prosecuted.

Bills passed by the World Congress must be approved by at least two of the Presidents to become law, with the same checks and balances of the 2010 US Constitution relating to new laws.

The 32 Earth-planet Executive Counsel members (29 plus the 3 Presidents) are chosen for six years by secret ballot from sitting members of the World Senate who have at least one term tenure in the Senate, voted-on by both houses of the World Congress. Executive Counsel members will advise the Office of the Presidency and retain their Regional upper house membership and vote, but cannot chair committees.

The Office of the President has executive powers controlled by the Constitution, and fully controls a

Cabinet group to administer major governmental units and functions (that have career civil-service staff) in different service areas throughout the Earth-planet. (The Office of the President has powers similar to those of the 21st- Century US President, but those powers are modified on a cyclical basis by a computer model that adjusts certain laws to reflect the peoples need or tolerance for Presidential influence/power.)

Each Cabinet member is selected by the Office of the President with advice and consent of the Executive Council. Cabinet members must have at least five years work experience in managing the departments(s) under their control or other departments within the purview of each cabinet member, and may be replaced by a majority vote of either the Office of the President or of the Executive Council. Civil servants below the level of Cabinet Member will serve subject to a job-performance review every four (4) years. They must retire at age 70.

The Bi-cameral World Congress consists of a World Senate and a World House of Representatives. The Senate is made up of a man and a woman member (minimum age 40, with proven leadership credentials, with no first-or second generation family connection to the other Senator and only one of which may be an attorney) from each of about 131 physical-culture units (called Provinces) in the thirteen geographical Regions of the Earth-planet; each Senator is elected by direct vote of all adults in his/her Province for eight years (staggered to overlap 4 years). The Vice-President serves as the chairperson of the Senate but may only vote to break a tie in the Senate vote. The Senate Information System is crypto-blocked from all other information systems and permits conferencing and voting from anywhere on earth-planet. Presidents and Senators are forbidden to leave earth-planet while in office. Senate controls own staff of computer systems analysts/auditors who are closely monitored.

The World House of Representatives

The World House of Representatives has about 2,000 members elected for four (4) year terms by adult voters in about 1,000 voting Districts within the (121–131) Provinces within the thirteen Region areas of Earth-planet. One male and one female Representative is elected from each District, staggered every two years. Each geographical Region, such as North America or South-East Asia, is divided into physical-culture Provinces based roughly on population but considering the matter of ethnic uniformity within each Province.

A Province may be politically influenced by certain tribal, language or religious groups, in which case the District boundaries within a Province may be designed by the Executive Council to break-up the cohesive power of such tribes, language groups and/or religions. Voting Districts are required to be simple square or rectangular as much as possible to prevent the old practice of 'gerrymandering'.

Each Representative is elected by all voters in his/her respective District, which may contain between about two and three million registered voters. Count of registered voters based on audited Voter Information System used by Representatives and field-Escorts, controlled by Senate President and audited by Senate computer auditors, validated where possible by census results.

Apportionment of District boundaries done by staff reporting to Chairperson of Executive Council every six (6) years based on latest counts on Voter Information System and validated by periodic census.

Representatives in each District are served by a large group of Escorts (and Escort Managers) under his/her control, each of whom provides personal response, information, and continuing personal service to about 6000 registered voters. A custom and very secure Voter

Information System (VIS) connects Representatives to each Escort in their group using computer terminals and/or other secure electronic technology. This multiplexed Information System provides each Escort with facts and information concerning pending and passed legislation, political, economic and social data... and anything relevant (each voter's personal representative-contact). In addition, the two-way VIS gathers advice, complaints and information on voters from the Escorts, as well as a tally of voter response on all matters, including officially tabulated votes on all matters. This Voter Information System is very secure and has the power of a legal document in all matters. It is subject to a very strong audit system outlined below.

Escorts are selected and trained from local communities as paid government workers. They are closely monitored, and act as official contacts of the related Representative in influencing and gathering information to and from voters. Escorts have no power over actual votes, which are cast in secret on local terminals of the official VIS computer system.

About 250 Escorts for each Representative communicate with and are controlled by the Voter Information System. Representatives send and receive summary information as needed to the Voter Information System, making direct contact with individual Escorts (and voters) as appropriate. In this way one Representative may serve about 1.5 million registered voters. (In 2010, about 550 US Representatives each serve about 600,000 voters using paid human assistants.)

Escorts are the more accessible direct contact with voters, who depend on the Escorts for political and economic advice as well as with contacts with other local governmental agencies and services. The Escort may contact Escort Managers and other Escorts of the same Representative in order to gain a stronger voice in influencing that Representative. A group of 100 motivated Escorts may move past the Representative to appeal directly to the Speaker of the House on any matter, including the introduction of new legislation. Representatives may message or contact Escorts, any voter or group of voters as necessary, but only using the monitored computers of the Voter Information System. Other contacts are controlled and publicly recorded. Unrecorded contacts, however innocuous, are an illegal prison offense. Escorts may be replaced by a related Representative with explanation to related voters.

Under a stable political and economic system Representatives are well-paid to work 16-hours per week from their homes or at the Congress center. The Voter Information System provides all their information needs, whether summary data or detailed and direct contact with any one or group of Escorts, other Representatives and members of government and/or any one or a group of voters. Teleconferencing via the VIS makes unnecessary the physical movement of Representatives.

As envisioned, under a stable world system, law-making and other political activity will be reduced... much less expensive than systems in use in 2010.

Escorts will know local officials, and are trained to know who to contact when voters need assistance. For general-elections, Escorts cannot count votes or serve on Election Committees. Each Escort controls a securely-encrypted computer that is tied into the worldwide political network for disseminating information on laws, proposed laws and other government matters. Escorts may not run for other public office until 4 years have elapsed from their time of service.

Senate members are elected by individual voters without involvement of Escorts. New laws may be proposed to a Representative by individual voters with 5000 support signatures on a petition or by 10 agreeing

Escorts. Double those numbers demand agreeing action by the Representative. The computerized votes are tallied and presented by secure-computer to the responsible vote-official or Representative.

Escorts are appropriately elected, trained and paid stipends to spend 16 hours per week on communication devices or in person explaining legislation to voters, answering questions and seeking opinions (developing consensus) and providing or coordinating assistance. Escorts are required to record and closely follow the wishes of a majority of their voter contacts. Escorts are elected by their constituents for two-year terms, not to exceed five consecutive terms. They may seek election again after a four-year delay. Escorts may seek to influence each other via the VIS and may communicate through the VIS with Escort-group managers appointed by their Representative. All communication between Escorts, voters, and their connected Representatives must be through the computer VIS and is encrypted and permanently recorded. All such records are in the public domain and available to the press.

The world government now has stable laws covering most needs. All communications, meetings and balloting by Representatives may take place electronically, individually (in person) or through electronic conferencing, with records of communications available to the press.

The Earth-Planet Senate

The Earth-planet Senate is responsible for originating tax laws and laws relating to financial matters and supervising the world financial system, as well as approving laws passed by the Representative House. This is a full-time (15- hour per week) job. Their responsibilities earn them high pay.

A group of technical communications specialists, employed and paid by the Justice Department of the Office of the President, is responsible for examining the content of the Voter Information System which is used by Representatives to communicate with Escorts, to cast votes on laws, to tally the votes and opinions expressed by their related Escorts, and to communicate those results to all parties and to the press. The electronic Press is totally free from government supervision.

A corps of 1,000 professional full time auditors (auditing two Escorts per day for 200 days each year), 100 supervising auditors and 10 managing auditors, with the Senior Auditor reporting directly to the Executive Committee Chair, on-site examine the records of Escorts as well as monitor and evaluate all aspects of the computerized political system. Auditors are trained, paid and supervised appropriately to combat corruption, with their work fully open to the press. Auditors are rotated Regionally every four years.

Regional Congresses for the 13 Earth-planet Regions are similar in structure to the World Congress, but concern themselves with matters pertaining to each Region. The constitutions of all Regional governments are very similar, differing only in respect to the geographic differences between regions.

A similar but modified political and governmental system exists for each extra-terrestrial colony (lunar, space station, planetary or asteroid-based). Space Colonies outside the solar system are autonomous, but leave Moon-planet with Earth-planet legal charters and constitutions. Solar Colonies enjoy 'home rule' for most governmental functions in a Commonwealth relationship with the Earth-planet system. Each colony is granted a government charter, even though the colony may be initiated by a private corporation. A model constitution is developed as soon as the colony becomes viable, with an appointed

Governor as head of the local project in partnership with a subordinate corporate manager, and with a man and a woman voting representative in the World Congress selected by and reporting to the Governor.

A local well-armed constabulary for each colony is paid and controlled by the earth-based Department of Justice within the Executive Branch of World Government to control law-enforcement according to Constitutional provision and serve the public on many matters, including paralegal counseling and family counseling. A fully-armed space-ready military detachment of adequate size is based on earth within the Justice Department, groups of which make annual extended good-will visits to each colony in the solar system.

Auditors with rotating one-year assignments review all finances and political systems of each colony. Local Governors are responsible for and control education, law enforcement and living conditions in the colony. Corporate managers are responsible for mining production and manufacturing production, as well as energy and food production. No private police are permitted in the colonial corporate organization. Weapons are controlled.

A division of the Judiciary reporting directly to the Office of the Chief Justice controls all computer programs in the VIS and political system, and all such programs are periodically re-written from tested modular blocks of officially certified computer code. All computer code modules are centrally generated, encrypted, and certified by a team of computer technicians, computer-literate attorneys and computer-trained special investigators. High standards of program simplicity and code understandability are demanded of each program used. All programs are open to periodic examination by qualified computer auditors and by members of the Press. Code is generated in each program to continually monitor the internal system for computer hackers, viruses and other criminal activity. The VIS is completely redesigned and re-written every 20 years using the latest standards of sophisticated controls.

The criteria for simplicity and internal code documentation in the programs and overall system is that any fully-trained auditor can understand and test the internal details of each program module in the system within four hours of examination. Code that cannot be so understood is rejected by that auditor with written justification and sent back to code technicians for re-write.

A group of roving-examiners which reports to the Attorney-General of the Executive Branch and whose reports are open to the press does at least one monthly surprise detailed-examination of anything they please.

The World Defense Department (under a Cabinet officer) controls a small mobile Earth-planet multi-function military force to support Regional governments in times of emergency. Within this force, there is a group of senior officers trained as mediators and arbitrators charged with settling disputes in any Region, with military support as necessary. A large Defense research program is focused on space-ship development and exploration, peace-keeping, and advanced weapons projects (with Congressional oversight and budget control by the Senate) for planetary defense. Each Region maintains a part-time military Guard program to help during emergencies, support the constabulary and to train persons for the World-force.

The 13 political Regions of the world are organized to minimize the effect of traditional tribalism. Known tribes are split between two or more Districts within political Provinces, with representation based on the numbers within each District. The laws themselves are designed to limit the complexity of government. Fees for attorney services are fixed by law within Regions.

The 13 Political Regions are designated to maximize political cohesion within a region, and to maintain North American leadership for the first 50 years. The Political Regions are self-explanatory:

1. Canada/US–defined by a line across present border between US and Canada, cutting SE from Detroit to Norfolk.
2. Mexico/US–defined by all land south of a straight line from Houston to Portland
3. Central US–All the rest.
4. North Europe, Greenland, Ukraine
5. South Europe–France, Spain, Monaco, Italy, Slovenia, Croatia, Bosnia, Albania, Greece, Turkey.
6. Pacific Basin (incl. Japan, Guam, Philippines, Australia, New Zealand, Galapagos, Hawaii).
7. Caribbean–including Central America, Columbia, Venezuela, Guiana
8. South America
9. Africa–all
10. Euro Asia–Russia, Belarus, Armenia, Kazakhstan, Turkmen, etc.
11. East Asia–China, Mongolia, Taiwan, part of Siberia.
12. South Asia–India, Pakistan, Indonesia, Malaysia, Thailand, Vietnam
13. SW Asia–Jordan, Syria, Arabia, Iraq, Iran, Afghan.

Geographical re-districting of political Regions every fifty years, by public vote of all Regional Congresses, each Congress having one vote.

Cultural Provinces within the 13 major Regions total about 131 (between 121 and 141) and have their own constitutions and elected mono-cameral legislatures and are headed by a popularly-elected two-person (man and woman) Province Advisor-Office and one vice-Advisor (elected by Provincial Representatives) who must break any deadlock between the two Advisors and who replaces disabled Advisors until elections may be held. An Advisor 's term is six years, and the vice-Advisor term is 3 years or less if replaced by the legislature (same gender for no more than 3 terms).

Districts within each Province, as far as possible reflect ethnic group origins. Representation in the World Congress is based on population and culture, with Representatives coming directly from and residing-in the Provincial and District areas.

The underground mining communities of the South and North Polar Regions (around 200,000 under-ground-dwelling miners, their families and other persons, as well as the surface-dwelling native peoples north of the Arctic Circle) are a single Autonomous Region with jointly one Senator and two Representatives (split male and female), but with no vote on Regional re-districting.

The Office of the Judiciary

The Office of the Judiciary is administered by three senior experts in Constitutional law with equal powers, with at least ten years Regional Court and four years World Court experience who are chosen from World Court justices by the World Congress after recommendation from the Office of the Presidency (by two out of the three presidents). Seventeen World Court justices, a man or a woman from each of the 13 Regions, two from colonies and two at-large lady-justices, have lifetime appointments and are selected by the Office of the President with advice and consent of the Senate from sitting Regional Court justices who have ten years judicial experience and who have taught in university graduate programs in Constitutional law with at least one refereed publication on the subject.

The group of Regional Court justices in each Region elects a judicial administrator from their midst, who shall have passed with honors graduate training in judicial administration. They also select and review judges from lower courts to fill vacant Regional Court posts with ten-year terms. They also select from their midst a 3-person life-tenure judicial review group which will investigate and impeach miscreant judges from their midst or from lower courts, said persons being no longer active judges.

Political B: War & Insurrection Prevention System

The War/rebellion Prevention System continually monitors all Regions, Provinces, Districts, cities and colonies. Professional assets (agents) and electronic monitors closely monitor non-integrated areas, reporting directly to related Regional governors.

Insulated areas containing remaining autonomous religious/political units are maintained free from human exit or entrance. Regional governments control all contact and trade.

Actual Earth-planet insurrection or terror activity causes massive insertion of Earth-planet Security forces, with all convicted combatants and their immediate families (including mobile parents) removed for re-training on Moon-planet with eventual colonial re-assignment. District government civil-service officials in insurrection area removed for re-training/re-assignment. Taxes increased on District to pay for 5-year Security Force intervention over 20-year period. Terror/insurrection membership tried and sentenced for personal illegal actions. Leaders banished to Pluto.

Political C: Variable Power Module

Automated System for Central Power Control (ASCPC) only system debate-senior to Earth-planet Constitution. Quiet and stable times, adjust more power to Earth-Congress for expanded democratic process. Trouble/stress times modify laws (Constitution) to move power more to Executive Office of President for strong leadership. Senior

Senator group can debate ASCPC decision with Supreme-Court decision-judge arbitration.

Lane 4: 2180, Earth-Planet Educational Systems

We have population control to know family size per population center and required economic and education infra-structure. We know which children will be learning what subjects in when time period. We give trained-counsel to all student and family; special learning counselor, family-planning counselor, wide-grin counselors and reproductive-assistance centers, tax levels to reward small families and tax penalties for spreading added social expense of very large families.

Education–schools teach strong pollution avoidance, forest/sea enjoyment and outdoor recreation, social tolerance, wide-grin and family-building and basic knowledge for productive living.

Children's happiness depends on play-access and stable family. There are many secure parks and play-areas next to living-homes. School-Students of age 4 to 13 live at home… in local school they are kept busy/happy with group study, field trip and sport for all. Lozenge-based, Telepathy-oriented or computer-based learning course-teaching where possible. A teacher/counselor for each student. Special programs for talented scientific students.

Older students to age 17 live-in central schools and are kept active with job-skill training, advanced sports and social training and wide-grin training/family planning. Projects and group study and field trips to work site. A difficult age: close-counseling for grooming, emotional problems, tolerance, teamwork, anti-social and aggressive behavior. Special programs when necessary for students.

Two-years public service is required of all students age 17 and 18. Career-related specialized training is available on a selective basis to all persons over age 18. Continuing education in most fields is available to persons throughout life.

Scholarship-supported university training for selected high school students.

Child behavior-pattern of violence or rebellion monitored in schools with personal counselor assigned to work with child and parents. Education on peaceful change methods for all students. Problem cases assigned to special units in High School system and incorrigible older-students moved to Space Security Forces for further off-planet training.

Lane 5: 2180, Earth-Planet Market-Based Economic System

Since the year 2100, private enterprise laws have favored small business with under 20 employees. Larger corporations are government monitored-stabilized but still viable and a major source of taxes and interplanetary investment. Management is now under strong control of Boards of Directors, all now held legally responsible for corporate actions. Judge-controlled Legal boards now control law suits and lawyer activity with power to mandate binding arbitration. Most businesses relate to interplanetary development or social services. Investment and banking is closely monitored by government to control risk-taking. Normal businesses are free to take all risks they wish in order to promote innovation.

Food production is now of great importance, due to reduced cropland caused by climate change. All agricultural chemicals used are proven safe or banned by government. Child-destroying chemical pollutants in food and environment were removed in 22nd Century.

Agricultural robots do most of heavy work in farming. Land distribution, aerial and ocean farming is government monitored to maintain the food supply (and prevent rebellion). Feudal power of large land-owning families that dominated economies of different countries was broken-up during 22nd Century after many local conflicts.

Manufacturing is automated and robotized to the extent that it is a minor employment factor.

Paid employment positions now include: police-persons, security monitors, massage specialists, recreation advisors, education teacher/counselors, personal counselors, family counselors, technologists, transport workers, equipment repair, small business and project managers, entertainers and artists, business and investment consultants, government workers, medical professionals, military professionals, nurses, sex therapists and wide-grin trainers. In a stable population environment, much construction and manufacturing is robotized or limited to the replacement market. New construction is robotized including planning and design, as well as the new-construction phase of replacement building, since robots are now programmed to make and read plans and perform all tasks according to building codes.

Any financial activity that focuses on economic expansion is closely monitored by government, to avoid over-activity that will precede recessionary collapse. Economic activity is computer-monitored to prevent inflationary investment-bubble.

Lane 6: 2180, Earth–Planet Language/Religion

Your visit to Earth-planet is an important part of effort to inculcate the Commonspeak language system in all colony-communities in the Sun-star region. Language and religion conflicts of 21st Century showed us that all must speak/feel the best modern communication methods.

The Commonspeak system that uses the fullest written, spoken, Icon-telepathic and Emotion-sensitive messaging (with full body-language) is the result of many-generations of language development… with communication design that is stable for next millennia. Commonspeak system acceptance on Earth-planet has been stable for three generations. Reconstruction after language and religious conflict on Earth-planet was completed by the year 2120.

Now, Earth-planet communication is standardized for all. Archaic-Local-language use is not school-taught and is permitted only in home of family and among immediate blood-relations.

Religion fully Constitution-free.... crazy-nuts OK, but no acceptance of religious murder, mass-murder or mass-suicide, and no religion-based child-rape/sodomy or child-slave/mutilation or religious-political activity/ insurrection tolerated. Most regions on earth-planet are free to worship as they wish with no political connection, however, there still are some fundamentalist regions which are not integrated.

Collapse/Chaos System

Seeing eventual collapse of historical systems into chaos, war, revolution… we did design collapse warning model to predictively evaluate all major plans and programs in government and private sector. System self-monitors all human interaction and attempts at modification. System has no destructive power. It can only send an 'Alarm-bong' icon and related data to all Earth-planet news media.

External Attack/Unplanned Event Module

Tamper-protected system to plan and develop protection to assure civilization continuation in case of difficult-to-foresee events.

Innovation

1. New forms of energy: The Energy Revolution covering the past two centuries has been based on

totally new forms of energy. Man has learned how to convert thought-energy into physical action, and to project thought across space and time.

Several levels of sub-conscious energy have been shown to emanate from the brain and can be consciously controlled.

Most electrical power now comes from 1) plasma-heat generators imbedded near hot mantel of earth several miles below surface of earth, and 2) downloaded via microwave from huge grids of solar cells now floating in space near earth (and most colonies), and 3) traditional wind and water power. The location and form of the space-grids also controls earth weather and rainfall patterns.

2. Brain functions are found to be based on a new form of electronics. This allows learning to be programmed using chemical-electronics. Brain aging is controlled, with brain segments and other organs being replaceable with bio-electronic cloned units. Greatly extended life is possible, for those who can afford to pay for the expensive research and memory loads. Great leaders are important enough to be given exceptional life span. Mental attitude is a function of programming. Happiness-level can be chosen and stabilized.

3. Now full-use on-demand of personal recreational stimulation device, developed over the past 50 years, to provide full nervous system and emotional experience for viewer (limited only to physical harm, but including all full-body artistic, rhythmic, action, wilderness, adventure and pleasure sensations, with extra-cost user-controlled variable imagination enhancement, fantasy storey extension and selected physical

stimulation enhancement including smell, taste, body-part, visual periphery and inner-ear dizziness/falling/flying sensation) of specially developed and directed multi-dimensional audio/visual magnetic media for private home use (guaranteed to keep the kids and relatives occupied). Expensive. Individual addiction danger: use only in small group.

✳✳✳✳✳

This description of a utopian world system can be further carried on to whatever detail is necessary for successful implementation.

We now consider the steps necessary to build a bridge toward implementation, the beginning of which must be in the time period 2020 -30.

9

THE DECADE 2150–2140

Using Backward Utopian Iteration (BUI), we move backward from the ultimate utopian goal of our program which we hope to realize by the year 2180 (Chapter 8), to a time period that is 30 years earlier. We derived the 30 year interval by dividing the estimated 150 years development time into 5 steps of 30 years each. As we further refine our plans, we may create more steps or change the estimated completion date.

In this chapter we identify those aspects of our civilization which have reached a steady optimal state and those aspects which are still undergoing development. Using the B.U.I. method, **IF** we can get from the beginning to this next-to-last step in the improvement of our civilization we will probably get to our utopian goal by 2180.

Progression from the World System that is now in place (in year 2120) to that which is planned for the year 2180 is the subject of annual and ten-year evaluations by the Executive Council 'Committee on the Future' of the planet and colonies. This formal study compares the goals set for civilization in the 21st Century with progress that has been made in all areas of the culture. From this review process, it can be concluded that earth civilization is stabilizing and progressing toward desired goals.

Where must we be in our plan by 2150 to have a high probability for attaining our goals for 2180?

Lane 1: 2150, Cultural

On the Earth-planet, things are quite normal . Everybody is getting richer, even though no one has to work much. There are a few poor around, but they are fishing and drinking beer. A terrorist crept out of an insulated area, but a monitor picked her up in two hours and they escorted her back. She was just curious about the outside. Reza's warts came back. It may rain this afternoon. Normal.

In the period 2150–2140 CE all Earth-Planet is focused on off-planet colonial development. There is huge excitement over a recently discovered asteroid that is about 40% quantium and silver. Kids on Earth pick rock-piles and name them for asteroids which they attack and defend like the old 'Nazis and Ruskys' game.

Twice each day down the incoming chutes of the several 18km-high space-docking Kaiser-needles, come bags of riches from the solar-system and asteroid colonies... exotic spices, gold, exanthium nodules, high-quality ponder-bash, medicines, rubies, and platinum.... and hundreds of universal micro-robots from the new Apple plant on the Earth-Moon. The four+ billion Earth-planet residents simply have everything... and they are always complaining.

Emigration to large industrial colonies on the moon and in giant space stations has eliminated population pressures on earth. The Earth-moon is a major manufacturing area, since the moon's low gravity allows low-cost space- transport to earth Kaiser-needles and to other planets and space-stations. Also, the Moon's lack of atmosphere allows efficiency in electricity production from solar-cell fields and nearby space-sail solar electrical units.

Limited water found in minerals on the moon is being used with careful conservation. Water is being produced using the ample electrical power to combine hydrogen and oxygen found in rocks. The hot core of the moon is also being tapped to produce lithium-plasma power. Heat cells that were developed during the last Century are being used to convert moon-core heat directly to both alpha and delta electricity. Dense bundles of these heat-cells are lowered into shafts penetrating into the moon's core… which transfer electrical energy in the form of microwaves to transmitters located at intervals in the shafts from the surface… and thence to the surface of the moon. Excess delta energy can be exported via mega-micro 'Blazewave' to the earth or other space stations.

Existing moon-caverns have been enlarged and sealed to allow habitation and farming to be developed in created atmosphere and light. They depend on adequate water production. Giant machines, made on the moon from parts produced in many planetary colonies, are creating caverns that are 50 km long and more than one km wide. These machines bore-out the moon rock and process it into mature soil which they lay to a depth of one meter behind, over a grid of future communication conduits and a grid of drip-watering systems. Water vapor and carbon dioxide are harvested from the artificial atmosphere at the upper levels of the caverns for re-processing into water and plant nutrients. Plant fertilizer is produced directly from rocks on the moon.

Millions of argon-xenon-matrix lights are embedded into the roof of the caverns with filters to produce soft light for plants that is optimum for 22-hour growth (with two hours of necessary partial darkness) for each artificial day…. but which is free of the damaging rays that age human skin. The roof of the cavern is not visible to those below, since each light appears as a twinkling first-magnitude star… nearly as bright as the brightest star visible from earth-planet. Light at the floor of the caverns is that of a normal sunny earth-day. The system can be modified to produce a 'daily' water downpour somewhat similar to earth-rain. This may be pleasant for humans and moon-dogs, but it is not as effective as the subterranean drip-water system for plants. A matrix of laser power units provides power to these lights without use of cables (developed as the first moon colonies were established).

Industrial facilities are mostly on the surface of the moon in domed structures that are designed for each industry. Human habitations are in nearby air-sealed tower structures which provide splendid views of the surrounding heavens (and earth) for all residents. Multiple floor-levels of businesses serve the needs of all residents, with parks and lakes on the domed ground-level.

Industrial domes are connected to residential towers by tubes containing high-speed human conveyors. While the automated industrial facilities are mostly run by robots, some human supervisors and maintenance personnel are required. These younger humans and their families live in nearby towers, which also contain shops, schools, medical facilities and offices. The majority of human residents of the towers are retired persons from earth-planet who have come to the moon to enjoy a longer and more healthful life permitted by the low gravity of the Moon......excellent for healing hemorrhoids and varicose veins.

While moon surface space is nearly inexhaustible for retirement towers, some regions are getting crowded enough that persons are choosing to move further out to Mars-planet, where living costs are lower. Occasionally moon residents are angered by a new tower that partially blocks their view of the Earth-planet. Some residents prefer the marvelous views of the galaxy on the dark-side of the moon.

Small underground colonies on Mars, in the ice on one of the moons of Jupiter (Titan) and on several asteroids are nearly self-sustaining but at primitive levels of hand-manufacture and subsistence farming in artificial atmosphere and light. Some colonies have failed, with the loss of all hands. Space-resident police have restored rule of law in more than one colony.

The decades-long effort to cool part of the surface of Venus is showing signs of progress. Cloud-generation equipment (made by GE on the nearest space-station) is functioning at the Venetian poles, and a huge Sony heat conversion net is blocking some of the heat of the sun and creating a surplus of beta and gamma electrical power to help future colonists in their xenon-plaster refrigerated soft-surface transporters get quickly into multifactor-cooled manufactured caverns under the surface on Venus. A similar pilot project on the hotter planet Mercury will be soon restarted after two disastrous attempts.

Earth-Planet

Without much to report, Earth is nice. Quality of life in the stabilized mid-size cities on land is lovely and peaceful. Pocket opera companies continue to develop, as well as quarter-symphony orchestras that use a combination of recorded and musician-made sound to create beautiful classical music. These provide exciting venue for rural or small-city artists and musicians who would otherwise be unable to use their talents. Many bars and nightclubs provide venue for myriad 'fire-music' groups.

The trend toward doming (building domes) is continuing in temperate and tropical cities, with many choosing to live roofless or under palm-frond roofs under the controlled-weather domes.

Earth continues to become a semi-agrarian planet, since former deserts are now lumber-producing forests and farms… and even former large cities have been broken up into extensive private garden areas. Battery and solar- powered transporter vans continue to be privately used by certain professionals and businesses, but most deliveries and human movement are by public underground tube or levitated transport.

Lane 2: 2150, Environment

With the Earth-planet environmental system stabilized after centuries of turmoil, focus is now on developing the environment of the Moon and other colonies. Major construction is taking place with the hollowing of giant Lunar caverns. Each major cavern is being developed with its own eco-system… with farms, forests, lakes, and parks for food production and human recreation. Farms and forests are tended by specialized robots that are centrally controlled by computers and monitored by humans. Controlled pollination is done by Micro-soft micro-drones. Human habitation is very limited on the floor of the caverns. The walls of the caverns are honey-combed with residences for humans who are involved with the productive ecology of the caverns.

Unfortunately, the earth may have begun the next glacial period, which may last thousands of years unless modified. Record snowfalls on north and south poles have exceeded expectations from efforts to reduce ocean depths by increasing polar ice. Glacier-level accumulations of snow (something over 70 meters–about 200 feet in thickness) are rapidly appearing. Old glaciers are rebuilding and expanding over the earth.

Construction has continued to install giant hydrogen-ion rocket engines around the equator of the earth, with the objective of slowing the elliptical orbital movement of the earth away from the sun in its multi-thousand-year glacial cycle. The engines are being fired sequentially as the earth-spin moves them into position to oppose the orbital progress away from the sun. Since there is much ocean at the equator the ion-engines must be placed as near as possible to the equatorial line on whatever land is available.

Since glaciers may eventually force the abandonment of northern surface-cities, new Tower-Cities are being developed on wastelands to the south of the 35thparallel north latitude (about the latitude of St. Louis) which was approximately the southern terminus of previous glaciers. Floating cities and undersea cities, like New Washington, are being built in the Mediterranean, the Gulf of Mexico, near Santa Barbara and Monterrey, near Taiwan, Guam, Hong Kong, and the Sea of Japan. An investigation into the tragic sinking of the floating city near Honolulu has just begun.

The existing network of thousand-square-km space energy-gathering sails is being adjusted to gather solar wind and focus the newly discovered Omega-factor electric power to earth to help increase ozone and carbon-dioxide in the atmosphere… and therefore reduce glacier-related cooling.

Lane 3: 2150, Political

The global political system was developed in the 21st Century and implemented during the last 60 years. All political boundaries have been eliminated except for those of several recalcitrant political-religion insulated areas. Regional wars and police actions have been avoided through arbitration under the supervision of the World Council. Civil insurrections have been settled after some damage. Population movement is unrestrained (except for insulated-unit residents), up to the limits imposed by population-balancing models that were developed in the 21st Century.

The political system at this time is immature and still being refined. However, the major features of the 22nd Century political system are in place. Political Regions, Provinces, and most Districts have been established and accepted by the populace. Negotiation and arbitration are being used to establish some Districts which have ethnic problems. The organization of government is functioning and radical differences have been settled. Representation has been accepted. Successful elections have been held for the World Congress using the new computer-based communication system and the Escort-counselors. An Executive Council is in place and the Office of the President is filled with three equal Presidents and a Vice-President. The male Vice-President came-out to be gay. Nothing is perfect.

The Voter Information System is in the delta-testing phase and appears to be functioning as planned. An auditor found a 'trap-door ' in the software control system, which caused some fur to fly (programmer re-assigned). Got her (the auditor) a promotion. Other computer sub- systems are also functioning. Escorts for most Districts are on duty and voters appear to accept the system. Auditors have been trained and are working. Rules must be established on the number of marriages permitted Escorts, who's socially-oriented jobs are in high demand.

Regional governments have been formed in the 13 Political Regions on the earth. Regional Executives and Congresses are in place, with some former nations still clinging to old legislatures. In most cases, those legislative members have been moved into the World Congress by election. There are dissonant voices, but no rebellion. With much work, there is a feeling that the system will carry the stable world population into the distant future.

The organization of the 127 Cultural Provinces is completed, with much trouble. Different states have argued against division or being excluded from certain desired political relationships or Regions.

Also, the possibility of glaciation in the next Century has caused population movements toward the south.

Korea had the choice to be a part of the Oceanic Region, along with Japan, or to join with greater China in the East-Asian Region. They chose the East Asian Region, with China and Taiwan. China was pleased to be joined with part of rich Siberia in East Asia, even though the ice is moving south. Several small mining cities in Northern Europe and Siberia have moved underground in reinforced caverns (the ice is very heavy) and are connected by deeply buried train-tubes.

Post civil-war French Provinces have voted to join with other South European countries. Most of France's Algerian survivors have moved back to north Africa, with financial subsidies from World Congress. The destroyed city of Paris has been partly rebuilt as a museum/university center and national park, with most of the survivors moving south or into the new undersea Provincial center near Brittany.

Many of the great paintings and statues of the Louvre museum were damaged in the conflict. The old centers of Lyon, Toulouse and Marseilles were vacated in the last Century in preparation for reconstruction. The new cities will be designed with large forests and park-lands within minutes of each new residential tower or business center. No privately-owned passenger cars will be permitted in the new cities.

In the last Century, the former nation of Turkey voted to join the South-European Region. The re-constructed former nation of Pakistan was placed in the South Asian Region along with India, Myanmar, Cambodia, Laos, Thailand and Vietnam. North America lost the Hawaiian group and other Pacific outposts to the Oceanic Region. Former US Admirals, focusing on primitive defense-in-depth concepts, protested new North American western borders at California and the loss of the Pearl Harbor naval base.

Among the insulated areas are the former Afghanistan (minus the Pashtun political District) and the western Kashmir. The political Provinces of former Pakistan are again stable, after civil insurrection Gaza-fallout reduced the population. Reconstruction began around 2030 CE.

Excess Earth-planet population is controlled through planetary migration. Family-planning education and government taxation on families with more than two children, as well as adequate retirement security has controlled population growth.

The development of the now 127 Provinces and related Districts around the world has taken most of the time of the Executive Council for decades. The careful balancing of cultural factors and political attitudes was most difficult. Reasonable success has been achieved. Surveys have been completed to establish simple geometric District voting boundaries and to develop laws to stabilize the decisions. District centers have been constructed as necessary. Troublesome 'gerrymandering' has been avoided.

Electronic communication (computer) equipment has been installed for the use of the newly elected and trained Escorts in all Districts. Regional voting has chosen all governmental officials in the World Congress and Regional centers. Voters have become reconciled to the election system with its small electronic devices, nearby Escorts, auditors, more distant Representatives and Senators, Regional Governors and congressmen and local officials. Business counselors and banks are assisting all levels of enterprise. Taxes are being collected and disbursed by government services.

The corrupt rule of many former countries by entrenched rich families has finally been broken, after considerable bloodshed. Land-reform programs are at last successful.

Autonomous colonies on some asteroids have demanded more independence and greater local control over industrial production. Some of the asteroids are wealthy enough to make strong demands on the Earth government. There is a fear on Earth that one or more of the space colonies will develop into a confrontational competitor, with power to make war. The Earth-Planet government is taking strong measures to prevent this. A planetary commonwealth system is developing.

Lane 4: 2150, Educational

Worldwide education is now based on computer-modeled thought recordings until age 13, when students are brought together for social training and more advanced work.

Research on brain-patterns and brain cell chemistry has produced an experimental lozenge/suppository which can inculcate specific blocks of learning directly into the cerebral cortex, making learning virtually automatic in certain basic areas. Testing of this learning-method must be carefully controlled for generations to ascertain possible brain damage.

The continued development of hugely powerful pinhead-sized matrix computers is causing a revolution in education. There is much resistance at all levels to potential trouble caused by the cerebral implantation of these devices in humans. The in-mind projection of these super-powerful I-pod-like devices has the potential to replace most education.

The stable political system is based on the social training of the educational system. Political science and the history of political thinking is taught in High School. Behavioral norms and responsibilities are taught from primary school. Different career fields and work patterns are also taught. Parental pleasures and responsibilities are taught, as well as work ethic and public service.

Lane 5: 2150, Economics

Earth-Planet regional political and economic systems are stable and developing well, according to the economic strengths of each region. Due to transportation expense and time delay, there is only modest trade in industrial goods with the planetary colonies. Even with the use of the new 18km Kaiser-needle, the volume of trade from Earth- planet to moon is not great. Still, thousands are using the Needle near Boston to assist their migration to the Moon. Electricity from the fast-moving Needle is powering much of Boston. The moon-based industries have a great economic advantage due to low gravity and cheap power, and are thus prospering.

High-value minerals and manufactured products from the moon (laser gear, robots, computers and solar energy equipment) are moving to earth on return spacecraft journeys after human cargos have disembarked.

The Moon colonies are also manufacturing and exporting technical equipment to other solar colonies for them to make rock-boring machines, and cavern-making, oxygen-making, atmosphere-making, light-making, soil-making, water-making, farming and mining equipment.

Earth-based economies tend to focus on goods for the earth markets, and are therefore geared to very slowly growing earth needs and the replacement market, with earth taxes and costs limiting profitability.

Progress is being made on a wage-free economic system based on standardized electronic credits related to service classifications. A new standard of customized incentives relates to each service classification. This system is designed to limit both riches and poverty.

Persons seeking riches are encouraged to migrate to more opportunistic colonies off-planet. Some planetary economies are experiencing huge profits and rapid growth based on technological innovation. Planetary taxes are kept locally, with emigration fees and investment interest covering planetary administrative costs. While colony industrial development and exploration may be under earth licensing and administration, public stock companies actually own most of the planetary colonial assets. They obtain profits from those investments, which are not subject to Earth tax.

Local colonial governments are managed by an Earth-appointed governor, and policed locally. Construction and production are managed by private corporations with government participation. Weapon control limits weapons on colonial planets. A mobile space police force maintains stations throughout the solar system.

Lane 6: 2150, Language/Religion

In 2110, a new system of communication, called Commonspeak began development under contract with the firm that simplified the English language. This will take into account both icon languages and alphabet-based languages. Thought-transferal and emotion communication is supplementing spoken communication in all but archaic cultures. Silent thought recording and playback was perfected in the 22nd Century. Feelings-based thought recording was developed in about 2140.

Religion has ceased to be a major issue. People think what they want, believe what they wish, move where they want and do what the law says they may. Freedom. Responsibility. Civilization. No war.

Iteration: Checking Our Work

For each Lane, we must look back at the previous chapter (our estimate of where we will be about 30 years in the future) at least one time to see if we have left out or neglected something important. Each subsequent chapter

(10, 11, etc.) is about 30 years earlier in time…. And
provides the basis for work in the later period. There must
be a logical progression in each Lane of endeavor.

THE DECADE 2120–2110

In the mid-22nd Century the planet Earth has achieved a unified, however imperfect political, social and economic system. Not all countries are fully cooperating, since there are still vestiges of the national sovereignty concept.... tribes willing to fight to the death to maintain their dominance over a special piece of land with little concern for the rest of the planet.

The greatest problems are being experienced by cultures that have been fixed in near feudal or tribal states for most of their history. Since nation membership in the Global Union is voluntary, each of these cultural units must be allowed to develop a plan for full or partial world integration depending on their perceived needs. Different levels of autonomy may be developed, as long as the external economics, communication skills and politics may be integrated with the world at large.

Lane 1: 2120, Cultural

The world has reached a stable cultural platform in most political Regions. However, there remain islands of resistance to world unification. The three North American Regions, working together with the European Regions, have the power to force total integration, but it is felt that recalcitrant populations can be persuaded to join the Global Republic given enough time. Some areas of total opposition have been insulated to protect neighboring peoples.

As usual, there are always the problems of population balancing, using taxes, wage rates, school/housing availability and job counseling to control some persons or groups that rush to any site where the opportunities seem better or the work easier. Anyone who really wants to become wealthy must go off-planet.

Lane 2: 2120, Environment

Old cities are being re-developed with private bank financing and governmental design subsidies into self-contained insular domed or tower communities of around 80,000 persons separated from other urban areas in a once-larger city by wide strips of forest land, parks and farmland that have replaced former streets and buildings. Much of the city transportation network is underground or 100–300 meters above ground. Traditional electric busses are still used in some areas where streets have been maintained for truck delivery. Highly taxed privately-owned solar-powered vehicles are still used in urban areas by certain professionals who require them for their work. Sealed towers and domes are used to control air quality and temperatures. Each 80-storey tower complex contains all facilities, shopping centers and services of an entire city along with view-residences for six-thousand families... sixty floors of apartments, twenty per floor in each of five towers.

Lane 3: 2120, Political 1

At this point, everything has been done to implement the new World Congress political system. If full preparation for this time had not been made during the past Century, the system would now be collapsing. Now there is nothing more to do than hold on and continue refining the various programs, looking forward to stability. Ahead of us lie years of fine-tuning, of putting-out fires, training, reviewing, cajoling, threatening, mediating, arbitrating. Civil insurrection and some police actions have greatly damaged some former nations. Generalized war has been avoided.

The many countries that have been dominated by greedy wealthy families have been most difficult to free from their determined entanglements of corruption. Typically, these families have seen their continuing growth in wealth and power at the expense of huge numbers of poor to be their only goal. Corruption in legislatures and courts have become traditional, with the objective of preventing the passage and implementation of reform legislation and effective constitutions. Only direct pressure, and occasional military intervention, from the North American-North Europe Commonwealth has changed these systems which enslaved the majority of their people.

Controlling rich families was once a problem of the old country called Mexico before integration with a North American Region. The wealthy family leaders often refused to see the poverty of their peoples until revolutions or civil war collapsed their systems… killing multitudes and endangering the rest of the world.

One of the most difficult steps was the first one: the establishment of 13 political Regions in the world. These had to be set up tentatively, since some Muslim states were not ready to cooperate at all and other nations were both reluctant to give up their sovereignty and at the same time wanted to be combined with other weaker nations that they could dominate. Since the North American Commonwealth had grown into a league of some sixteen nations on two continents, it was in a position to arbitrate according to the original Regional plan. It has been renamed World Commonwealth.

Some modifications in their thinking have brought the world of political religions closer to the mainstream of the world community. Some areas with dominant Muslim populations have begun to integrate and cooperate. These programs involved huge educational effort... to modify and liberalized religious attitudes and practices and to teach employable skills to the people.

Lane 3: 2120, Political 2

Continued development of constitutions and continuing improvement in physical political organization is occurring as new countries and regions join the World Commonwealth. Standardized constitutions have been developed to cover many of the needs of the different developing Provinces and Regions... being modified as necessary by the economic geography and political history of regions.

The political organization of the Moon colony, planets and asteroids within the solar system has become important. Migrations to these rich planetary units has absorbed most population increases on earth. Large space stations are also important, since they may be placed more advantageously in relation to the sun. Such a station can provide power transmission from space energy systems to earth and also for an extensive maintenance operation of all types of space equipment... satellites, solar energy gathering and solar wind units, as well as space manufacturing units and space-craft docking and launching.

The Moon has become a large retirement center The fantastic views of earth and stars has a rejuvenating effect on residents of the Moon, where there is no atmosphere to pollute. It is also now a large manufacturing center and a transportation center for shipment of goods to earth, other planets and space stations... as well as a source of high-value minerals for earth.

Lane 4: 2120, Education

During this period, developments in Simple-English communication are replacing traditional English as a language. Research has simplified and clarified the language so it is easier to learn while not diminishing the communicative value of the language.

Work is underway to inculcate knowledge via substances that can be taken by mouth or inhaled that cause the brain to either be more open to learning and/or to directly acquire knowledge in the form of brain memory cell modification. In addition, the science of mental projection as related to telepathic icon communication has begun to create entirely new language forms. The decision was made to continue spoken language, however inefficient, but to blend it with telepathically projected emotional feelings and icon telepathy.

Migration to space colonies is a valid option at this time, and work opportunities in such colonies is attractive enough to provide migration incentive. Education must also support such employment.

Lane 5: 2120, Economy

Strong governmental control of the private financial system and economy continues, since the world community has not yet stabilized. Population is stable and population movement is declining. Investment in different regions of the earth has made living conditions in most areas similar in quality…. although perhaps different in terms of weather conditions and geography. Due to weather, many cities on earth are under air-conditioned domes or undersea.

There are now few industrial or manufacturing jobs on earth. Industrial robots are performing most tasks. Most of the roughly 5 billion earth population is employed in agriculture and service industries (including government at all levels). Investment in agriculture is recognized as important after a period of food shortages occurred during the last Century. Specialized farm robots are taking over much of the heavy work in farming.

Most trade is between earth regions. Trade with space stations and lunar facilities is small but growing, however, energy costs relating to pushing rockets out of the earth atmosphere remain prohibitive. Most trade in products and materials is one-way... moon to earth. People are moving out from earth to moon and other stations.

The Kaiser-Needle-2

A 20-kilometer-high space docking tower near the coast north of Boston, in the US. This tower, a thin column of a new high-strength steel-aluminum-titanium alloy containing fuel and human transport shafts will support a docking terminal in the stratosphere at about 65,000 feet... above 99 percent of the dense air, and will be moving at about 800 km (450 miles) per hour to the east (with no perception of movement, since it will be far above all weather). Space craft can approach from the west and never have to decelerate below 450 miles per hour to dock. Rocket launches to the east will start out at 450 miles per hour and avoid accelerating through the earth's dense atmosphere. The tower will be supported on all sides by cables similar to those used in a suspension bridge. Static electricity from lower (atmospheric) levels of the Needle will generate enough power to light much of Boston.

The tower might cost $500 million to build and save perhaps $10 million in fuel per rocket launch... paying for itself in perhaps one year at a rate of one launch per week. Space vehicles would be much cheaper to build if they did not need extensive heat protection for penetrating the earth's atmosphere to sea level.

A needle tower at the south pole has been considered, but the terrible weather would be a factor and the polar needle would not be as fuel-efficient for the rocket transporters. The existing Kaiser-Needle on Baffin Island in northern Canada cost less to build, since the tower is moving less rapidly through the atmosphere, but it's isolation near the north pole reduces its effectiveness.

The Bering Tunnel

The last link in the new Seattle–Beijing magnetic rail line proved formidable. The 9,000 mile run was nearly a straight line, going through Siberia and Alaska, and the train, running just under the speed of sound (about 740 mph at sea-level) was expected to make the trip in about 13 hours... hours faster than sub-sonic aircraft and at much lower fuel cost. Boring tunnels through the Canadian Rocky Mountains and the lower mountains of Siberia was no problem for the robot-driven boring machines.

But the 80-mile-wide Bering Strait (between Siberia and Alaska) would have added several hours if a normal jet-foil ferry was used.... which was not always possible in the stormy strait. A normal train tunnel, such as that under the 22 mile English Channel, would have been dug a few hundred feet under the sea bed, following the curvature of the earth. Instead, engineers chose to design the tunnel in an absolutely straight-line... ignoring the curvature of the earth.

This straight line between the two shores, at its deepest point, takes the triple-tube tunnel down to a depth of about 4 miles beneath the surface... close to the hot mantle of the earth... through rocks averaging about 160 degrees Celsius. After solving the problem of keeping the robot boring machines cool, the tunnels were dug in about eight months, at the rate of about one-quarter mile per day. The tunnels were then lined with spiral pipes to create steam from the hot rocks, which then generated enough electricity to power the magnetic trains for half the Seattle–Beijing distance. The straight line was also several miles shorter than the curved line, saving more than a billion credits in cost.

*****

All of the above areas of development are moving toward the goals set for the next level, at the decade 2140–2150.

Iteration: Checking Our Work

For each Lane, we must look back at the previous chapter (our estimate of where we will be about 30 years in the future) many times to see if we have left out or neglected something important. Each subsequent chapter is about 30-years earlier in time.... And provides the basis for work in the later period. There must be a logical progression in each Lane of endeavor.

11

THE DECADE 2090–2080

This Backward iteration stuff is getting a bit boring. this interim chapter just shows what we must do in this time period to prepare for the next step ... the decade starting 2120... which we covered already in chapter 10.

You might wish to skip this chapter and jump to chapter 12, where things do get nasty.... closer to the mess in the period 2015–40.

Having progressed as a world civilization through the year 2090, an increasingly stable and mature global human system will be expanding into the Solar planetary sphere.

Developments during this time period in social, political, economic and educational systems will continue progress toward those goals set for the decade starting 2120. Again, if we can meet the criteria we have set for this time period, we have a good chance of continuing progress to the next 30-year goals... and onward.

Lane 1: 2090, Cultural

The world is approaching a steady-state social system where the economic and social integration will be complete. This means that people are able to migrate across the earth, encountering few boundaries and little prejudice.

This must be supported by an in-place world educational system that provides all persons with knowledge they need to live a good life wherever they wish. While the unification of the world is not yet complete, total union is close enough to allow people to cross what boundaries exist. The problem of excessive population movement is controlled by using a lottery system to limit migration and destination. Educational and language standards are imposed on those wishing to migrate.

Migration to space colonies is a valid option at this time, and work opportunities in such colonies is attractive enough to provide incentive. Education also supports such employment.

Lane 2: 2090, Environment

Two new forms of energy, steam generated electricity from interior earth heat and gamma-molecular solar energy from large space energy-gathering grids have added to the many atomic reactors to return the seas to the level of the year 2000 by re-freezing the polar ice. This effort is creating large areas of farmland and future forest, ready after some years of de-salinization.

Giant engines using an ionic form of hydrogen are being built around the equator by the world community to begin the control of the earth in relation to the sun (by modifying its orbit).

Energy input to major cloud systems is continuing the control of storms and rainfall to turn more areas of desert into farmland.

Many older north-American cities have been re-developed into insular communities of around 50–80,000 persons separated from other urban areas by strips of forest land, parks and farmland. Much of the city transportation network is underground or 50–150 meters above ground.

Lane 3: 2090, Political

A continuation of the trend toward political union among all the countries of the earth. This era around 2090 is difficult, since some countries and regions of the world still resist integration with a world commonwealth that is lead by North America. There are competing groups of countries, such as the Mandarin-speaking region and the Russian-speaking region. Great effort is being made to provide economic incentives or otherwise motivate these people to expand education in English as a second language or in a new language that is a combination of English and other languages. English is simply too important a language for it to be discarded, but there is great language pride among humans.

Modifications in the Muslim program have brought that world closer to the mainstream of the world community. Some regions with dominant Muslim populations have begun to integrate and cooperate.

Continued development of constitutions and continuing improvement in physical political organization is occurring as new countries join the North American Commonwealth.

Much activity is taking place on the moon as a retirement center, since the low gravity eases the life of older people. It is also becoming a manufacturing center for shipment of goods to other space stations and a source of minerals for earth.

Lane 4: 2090, Education

There is a major revolution underway in educational research and technology. Major re-design has occurred at all levels of the educational process. Children are beginning younger and being taught a wider range of subjects. Older students are also learning a wider range of subjects and are being taught in new environments.

Education has become more demanding and more fun for all, including the teachers.

An entire new class of learning and social counselors has been trained and put to work, in an effort to teach all people how to be happier, or at least more satisfied, in their lives. While government is expected to become smaller and cheaper in the future, along with the military, education will require more people. In the future, as educational technology changes teaching, costs will be reduced. The number of teachers will be reduced. The number of schools may be reduced as young students learn at home or in smaller groups with less equipment… and older students will work together in live-in education centers. The need for counselors will remain.

Lane 5: 2090, Economy

Strong governmental control of the economy continues, since the world community has not yet stabilized. The economic needs of the world community will be quite stable and under control, since population is stable and population movement is declining. Investment in different regions of the earth has made living conditions in most areas similar in quality…. although perhaps different due to weather conditions. To control weather, many cities on earth are under air-conditioned domes or undersea.

There are few industrial or manufacturing jobs, with industrial robots performing most tasks. Most of the roughly 5 billion earth population is employed in service industries.

Most trade is between earth regions. Trade with space stations and lunar facilities is small but growing, however, energy costs relating to pushing rockets out of the earth atmosphere remain a problem. Most trade in products and materials is one-way… moon to earth. People are moving out from earth to moon and other stations.

Lane 6: 2090, Language

During this period, developments in communication have begun to replace traditional English as a language. Research has simplified and clarified the English language so it is easier to learn. Work is underway to inculcate knowledge via substances that can be taken by mouth or inhaled that cause the brain to either be more open to learning and/or to directly acquire knowledge in the form of brain memory cell modification. In addition, the science of mental projection is related to telepathic icon communication to create entirely new language forms. The decision was made to continue spoken language, but to blend it with telepathically projected emotional feelings and icon telepathy.

✳✳✳✳✳

All of the above areas of development are moving toward the goals set for the next level, at the time 2120.

At the End of Chapter 11–Iteration–Checking Our Work

For each Lane, we must look back at the previous chapter (our estimate of where we will be about 30 years in the future) at least one time to see if we have left out or neglected something important. Each subsequent chapter is about 30-years earlier in time…. And provides the basis for work in the later period. There must be a logical progression in each Lane of endeavor.

12

THE PERIOD 2060–2050

Disaster: The One Day Exchange of 2047

Bulletin: "Experts believe that Palestinian Gaza was destroyed accidentally in the *'One Day Exchange of 2047'*, since the atomic-missile ground-burst at Gaza caused intense radioactive fallout that killed most people downwind in Baghdad and elsewhere to the east of Israel. The missile launched from Iran was **probably aimed at Israel** as a low-fallout air-burst, but went astray due to the launch by untrained Islamist terrorists, exploding on the ground at Palestinian Gaza. No one was left alive in the north of the former country of Iran to confirm or deny the reports. Tehran was also in the deadly fallout pattern from the Gaza missile, but the former city is now part of the uninhabitable area that is all of the former northern Iran. Northern China, Korea, Japan, Seattle, Vancouver and Edmonton were also directly downwind (to the east) from Gaza, and were not prepared for the lethal fallout from the Gaza ground-burst."

The experts think that the six atomic-missiles fired in all directions by Iran after the perhaps terrorist-caused Gaza missile-launch was done to assure enough infidel (or Sunni Muslim) deaths to guarantee entry into paradise for all Shi'ite Iranian males. They could find no other reason for the Iranian missile strikes on

the (mostly Sunni) Muslim cities of Istanbul, Karachi
and Cairo. The television showed some people dancing
in the streets of Tehran because of the atomic-missile
strikes on Moscow, Jerusalem and Rome during the few
minutes before the counter-strike hydrogen-bomb missiles
from NATO, Russia and China arrived. Jerusalem was
successfully protected by anti- missile defenses. Moscow
was destroyed in spite of strong anti-missile defenses,
which were focused on protecting from a strike from the
west (European NATO). Russian planners never could
accept the fact of a dangerous Iran on their southern
border. A sense of relief in the West over the end of the
Iranian atomic missile threat was marred by furious
college- student peace demonstrations in America, who
fought police and firemen to a standoff while many
campus buildings were burned to ritual naked dancing
and the roasting of marshmallows. Sunni Muslims made
no comment concerning the demise of most of the Shia
Muslims. Perhaps they were envious that the dead Shi'ites
had achieved certain paradise. Most Europeans, except
the surviving Romans, were very critical of the rapid
hydrogen-bomb missile response of the North-American
coalition. They felt that a commission should have been
appointed before the missile counterstrike to investigate
and make recommendations on how to avoid further
'accidental' missile launches.

Moscow, Istanbul and Rome are being reconstructed,
but the ruins of Saint Peters in Rome will remain as a
shrine. No decision has been made concerning the ruins
of Karachi and Cairo, but the damaged Great Pyramid at
Giza will be rebuilt as a tourist attraction. The remainder
of the former Iran, a few villages in the south, are
insulated areas to be kept free of electricity, fuel and the
wheel.

Following the success of Iran in producing an
atom bomb against the wishes of the United Nations,

nuclear- control negotiations had broken down in 2031. But the US government had claimed the Iranian atom-bomb threat against Israel had been 'neutralized'. However, there was a known radical Muslim faction in Iran that saw an atomic war as the immediate path to paradise for all true believers. During the Iraq–Iranian War of the 1980s, this same group had also recruited hundreds of young boys that gained immediate martyrdom/paradise by running across mine fields ahead of attacking Iranian soldiers. It is known that some members of this radical faction were part of the Iranian atomic missile brigade. They may have illegally launched the atomic missile toward Israel that accidentally struck Gaza. All parties now claim the Iranians started the '2047 Exchange', since they had broken their promise to remove the atomic warheads from their missiles.

✳✳✳✳✳

In order to survive until the year 2060 as a viable civilization and progress toward the goals of 2180, we must have accomplished most or all of the following:

Lane 1: 2060, Cultural

The culture of the present United States has been re-designed thru improved education (and persuasive leadership) to accommodate the temporary infusion of many more Mexican people, their education and social acceptance. Many Mexicans are now able to compete with their northern cousins on an equal language and training basis.

The emotional backlash and political problems related to this movement of peoples in North America has required educational changes in school curriculums in order to prepare all people.

Problems relating to the competing or dissonant goals of North America, Russia, China, India, Brazil and other large countries have been solved by sharing, cooperation and positive leadership.

The 2047 Exchange was truly caused by indecisive US leadership in 2014 permitting Iran to make an atom bomb.

North America has become leader in reducing the tension between the Muslim world and the rest of the world. Decades of restricted out-migration, the 2047 Exchange and recent reduction in oil revenues has put pressure on Muslim peoples to reduce excessive birth-rates and may bring some to the conclusion that some political aspects of Islam are not compatible with the 21st Century.

A policy of restricted Muslim immigration is to be retained until such changes are certain. A strong radical Islamic sector in a few Muslim countries continues to justify caution. Continued pressure from the North American group has modified educational standards in the world of Islam to reduce the religious hatred formally taught some Muslim schools.

Lane 2: 2060, Environment A

The world has stabilized the more difficult environment created by 20th- Century lack of foresight. There are some on-going local conflicts being fought by peoples trying to relocate into already crowded areas of less ocean flooding and more food, such as northern Bangladesh, the area north of Karachi and the submerged Indus river delta where inadequate sea walls have exposed the people. The Amazon delta is partly submerged, killing huge areas of rain-forest which is now causing weather changes worldwide.

Sea walls are in place protecting most large ports with flood-gates and locks protecting large inland seas.... except the sea-gates at Gibraltar which have proved too large a project... with related flooding of ancient Mediterranean ports from Marseille to Istanbul, some of which failed to build protective sea walls in time. The Nile delta has also flooded, causing violent population shifts and famine. The Po delta flood gates collapsed during a storm, inundating far inland. Sea-related destruction of ancient treasures has cut tourism in the Mediterranean.

The unwillingness of some countries to spend some billions of dollars in reducing carbon pollution in the early 21st Century has cost the world many trillions of dollars in sea-wall construction and lost land values during the past forty years to defend against rising seas. Bankers, contractors and heavy equipment firms have profited handsomely. Jail sentences have been given to many who accepted bribes from polluting firms and land developers to delay enforcing pollution laws. Millions have had to relocate inland and many have died in the process.

Food production is down world-wide and there are areas of severe famine. Many rice-growing areas are under sea water, especially the Mekong and Yangtze river deltas and low-lying areas of Indonesia and the Philippines. Food costs are rising world-wide. Cotton crops have been reduced in the flooded Mississippi and Nile deltas, causing prices to rise in all clothing.

Rain-forest flooding in Brazil and Indonesia have increased storm frequency and severity world-wide. Much shipping has been destroyed, in harbors and at sea. Large storms still break through the sea-walls erected to protect coastal cities. Terrible storms in the North Sea have heavily damaged the walls protecting Hamburg harbor and the unfinished locks at the Copenhagen entrance to the Baltic Sea.

Ocean waters reached maximum increased depth of about 2.1 feet and have apparently stabilized.

Lane 2: 2060, Environment B

Carbon-based fuels have ceased to be a major factor in transportation. More compact cities have reduced the need for motor cars, which now all use batteries and/or solar power. In spite of continued concern over catastrophic risks, atomic power stations produce more than half of power needs. Solar power is increasing from large solar panels now floating in space near the earth. World rail systems have converted away from diesel power to electric. Truck tractors are larger and pull larger loads, using new cesium-7 steam engines supplemented by solar panels.

Local insurrections, the 2047 Exchange, disease and famine have taken their toll, and earth population is under 5 billion. The most serious losses occurred in Africa, which is still politically unstable.

Countries depending on oil export have raised prices and cut production, as oil reserves have dwindled. Falling oil revenues have depressed economies and destabilized populations in the Middle East. Increasingly violent storms have reduced oil output from off-shore oil fields. Gasoline, where available, now costs a world average of $19 per gallon.

Continued development of huge deposits of natural gas from oil shale and other sources has revolutionized the heating industry and made liquid petroleum stocks somewhat less critical in the transportation industry.

Fuel costs and related air-fare increases have reduced air travel and increased rail travel. New high speed rail lines are being built, with train speeds now averaging about 250 miles per hour on the new lines. Experiments are being conducted with a new design of magnetic-levitation trains which have a theoretical speed of twice the present high speed trains.

Lane 3: 2060, Political A

Russia and China are in disagreement over land use by both in Siberia, with the North Americans mediating. Russia is growing again in population, now near 85 million, after a period of heavy loss. China is still trying to cope with insurrection in sections of the country that wish autonomy.

There are about 60 million Chinese men who cannot find wives, some of whom may wish to migrate to Siberia. Polyandry, one woman having many husbands, and prostitution is increasingly practiced to avoid conflict among males over women, with a resulting increase in the wealth and power of women in China and India.

The European Union is still dealing with problems of integration, with a small number of western nations, led by Germany and France, now dominant. These powers are still unable to get some other union-members to fully cooperate. Some countries have left the European Union, due to financial and sovereignty disagreements.

Lane 3: 2060, Political B

The North American Commonwealth is prosperous and strong, having passed through a difficult period of nation-building between Canada, Mexico and the United States. The treaty combining the three countries was ratified after years of effort. French-speaking Quebec has also joined the North American Commonwealth with the question of language not yet settled.

Many in the US were upset with the abandonment of US sovereignty, and fear domination by the fast-reproducing Mexicans. There was equal resentment on the part of the Mexicans, who have seen their country bisected by the 'Yanquis' in the past. Massive investment in southern and central parts of the former independent Mexico has greatly improved living standards. Population movement to the former United States has stopped, with many now returning to good jobs in their native Mexican towns.

The political systems of the continent of North America are rationalized and organized for future improvements. New constitutions for the three major countries involved have been coordinated as a part of full political and cultural union. This is now a constitutional representative/participative republic with flexibility built-in to move from more authoritarianism and less democracy to more democracy and less authoritarianism, depending on a predictive control system.

Provisions of the Senior Constitution that was developed and enacted during the 2030s are open-ended, in that added partner-states may be added to the North American Commonwealth after acceptance by the Executive Group of the Union and after a ten-year period of cultural and political blending. The name will change from Amerimexican Union to North American Commonwealth when the Executive Group chooses. At this time, the Union consists of the original three nations plus the former United Kingdom, Germany, Poland and Sweden.

Lane 3: 2060, Political C

The goal has been set by North America to work toward **full political union of the entire earth in the next 200 years.** A planning commission is working on the huge political, constitutional, social and linguistic changes necessary. This union is seen as necessary as space colonies become a reality.

Lane 3: 2060, Political D

Efforts continue to reduce concentrations of restive Latinos in the former US southwestern states. People movements from the former Mexico northward are being directed further north and east. All schools in north America teach most classes in English. Other languages are freely permitted outside of public schools, but not encouraged. Laws protecting ethnic minorities and encouraging integration are enforced.

*****

Military expenditures have been reduced, with savings directed toward debt reduction. There are fewer Navy ships. While Navy ships are still needed to maintain control of the seas, they are now focused on aircraft carrier groups on station near south Asia and the Mediterranean and on missile and attack submarines.

A new Navy 'good-will' class of ships that was designed to provide emergency assistance to other ships at sea, control of piracy and rapid response to tsunami catastrophes is now patrolling all the oceans. These ships carry a store of emergency supplies and a portable field hospital as well as on board surgical facilities.

Army divisions have been reduced and Army forces stationed overseas have been reduced. Army focus is now on rapid-air-mobile forces, Special Forces, language and cultural training, goodwill building and intelligence gathering. Combat divisions are all air-mobile for rapid deployment anywhere... cold or hot weather.

Air Force heavy bombers have been replaced by missiles and lighter aircraft for multi-use. Focus of Air Force is on drone surveillance, heavy military transport, intelligence gathering and on the Space activities. Drones constantly monitor all areas of suspected insurgent activity on the earth. Close coordination is maintained with inserted Army Special Forces units and other observers. The expanded Marine Corps is fully trained, air mobile including new light tanks that ride on a cushion of air above the ground and helicopters with ground and air missiles, and is equipped for counter-insurgency.

Lane 4: 2060, Educational

Education continues to be the key to progress toward a better future. After decades of resistance, university professors have completed curriculum modification in support of the political and cultural thrust of the new systems. These changes came about only after student pressure, including some boycotts, forced them. University colleges of education have been most laggard in modifying curricula to support the new teaching innovations being introduced in primary and secondary education. Federal grants to support these modifications have been a key aspect of the program.

Lane 5: 2060, Economics

Land Reform in the former Mexico has helped to build a larger middle class, while minimally reducing the income of the already-rich feudal estate-owners. The break-up of large agrarian estates is proceeding slowly. Land reform laws have been strongly resisted by large plantation owners... forcing equally strong action from state authorities. Many nations of the earth, ostensibly democratic, are still rich-family controlled aristocracies. The elite families still control courts and legislatures in their countries and still are interested in only increasing their great wealth and power at the expense of poor people, whom they disdain, ... making the breakup of control dependent on pressure from the Amerimexican Union.

Tax reform in the North American Commonwealth has standardized tax rates, decreased tax crime and increased tax revenue…. being used to reduce debt.

A more mature and less aggressive North America will have the strength to assist these nations in seeking solutions to their own problems.

Russia, in particular, has needed demonstrations by North America of genuine support in their quest for regional suzerainty and defense-in-depth. Given their history, and the large external ethnic populations, this quest of the Russians is reasonable. In return, improved cooperation with the Russians has improved the world and reduced tensions. Agreement is in force to reduce atomic weapons to near zero.

Lane 6: 2060, Language/Religion A

Language is a major impediment to world political union. While no answer has been found for a common language for the world, English is the language of world trade, technology and the military. English has been greatly simplified and set on self-teaching equipment. One billion subsidized copies of self-taught simplified English discs have been distributed in Asia, with another 300 million copies to South America.

Lane 6: 2060, Language/Religion B

Based on wartime Presidential decisions, some Muslims who were not born in the North American Commonwealth have been returned to their land of origin with financial subsidies. This movement was voluntary, since Constitutional protections prevented mandatory movement. Some Mosques have been closed, minarets forbidden by some local building codes, face-covering forbidden as aiding criminals. Imams who preach violence against the Constitution have been restrained or deported.

A study has been made to determine if any Muslim countries have begun to moderate the tenants of their political religion to reduce the direct threats to liberal Constitutions in the world. Morocco, Turkey, Malaysia, Indonesia and some west African nations are being considered. Terrorist activity is being closely monitored.

Many persons with Arabic language, ethnic and cultural background have been trained in special forces techniques and inserted into Muslim nations as covert observers. The numbers of these persons is much less than the remaining Muslims in the West.

2060, World Systems

The Chinese/Amerimexican space station and moon landings resulted in greater cooperation in space development. Major mining operations on the moon have begun to pay for expenses. Existing space stations assist the moon operation. A major underground moon city is under construction. Plans are laid for more extensive mining and for launching colonies on other planets.

*****

A group of specialists in future systems monitors progress in the above areas every ten years and compares this progress to goals that have been set for the time period 2110 AD.

Iteration: Checking Our Work

For each Lane, we must look back at the previous chapter (our estimate of where we will be about 30 years in the future) at least one time to see if we have left out or neglected something important. Each subsequent chapter is about 30-years earlier in time.... And provides the basis for work in the later period. There must be a logical progression in each Lane of endeavor.

13

FROM 2030 TO 2016

The End of the B.U.I. Bridge:
What We Must Do to Begin…

We have come back to the present in thirty-year steps
from the goals we have set for a better civilization as soon
as possible…. which appears to be about 200 years in
front of us. In those ten or so generations, we must free
ourselves from some of the limitations of the present,
educate ourselves to be able to implement programs of
the near future, cope with the inevitable changes that
science, other 's political goals and the environment will
produce, install modifications to our social system and
amendments to our Constitution that will open the door
to political improvements, and plan the details of a better
civilization. To get started, we need to just turn-around
in our track and see the path we must take to our best
future…. without war.

But wait!

We are not quite finished. We still have the next 15
years to deal with. And they will be difficult.

It is possible that peer pressure from small groups
(that's you) using the Internet and other social media
can convince a nucleus of legislators to begin to push
for a system that is similar to that outlined in this book.
But sooner or later some leader must emerge to carry

the flag. What we will need is an explorer like Magellan or…. Captain Kirk, of Startrek… someone who is a good communicator and a clear thinker. …and a bit of good luck.

OK. Let's look for a decision-maker… a real leader, but NO dictators like Hitler, Stalin or Napoleon. We need a Margaret Thatcher… an Eisenhower…. Teddy Roosevelt. How about Oprah? Old George Washington? W. Bush? Obama? Mc Cain? Putin? Blair?

Wait. Go back. We've got Obama.

Well, he could be the one. But will he choose to? He has the smarts, the looks and the voice…. and an even better 'Jackie'. But will he?

It looks like all seven+ billion of us really come down to depending on one man to get us started. There's a crossroads for you. That is an awful lot to dump on one man, even if he is THE man.

President Obama…. what is in his mind? Of course, like ex-President Woodrow Wilson, Obama wants the history books to show him as a man of peace. Noble. He's already a Nobel laureate. But wasn't President Wilson's indecision, or perhaps it was a stroke, one of the direct causes of the rise of Adolf Hitler … and World War II? Indecision really IS deciding. Of course, Obama's childhood in Muslim Indonesia, recent apology to Islamists in Cairo and Executive Order admitting many Muslim Palestinian immigrants does not bode well for his unleashing the Israeli air force on Iranian atom-bomb factories. But who knows? We elected him President because he seemed decisive.

The Iranian atom-bomb program is important. They would like us to think they are stopping. But they are not. Just smoke in the stupid American's eyes. The same way North Korea got the bomb. Works every time! It takes a 'Pearl Harbor ' to wake up the Americans. Very soon their own Iranian atom-bomb will give Muslim Iran huge prestige… impressive new geo-political power in the Mid-East… and most of the Muslim world… even though their Shi'ite sect constitutes only about 18% of all Muslims. But Iran is known to sponsor terrorism, and has much use for the power of the atom bomb to intimidate other countries. This power may soon see Iran dominating Iraq and the oil production of the entire Persian Gulf… and even the Caspian Sea oil and gas on their northern doorstep… giving them control of most of Europe's energy needs.

They will get this power without even using the bomb to destroy Israel, as they have promised to do. How much time does this give Israel? ….Or Christian Europe?

Does Obama really desire that legacy?

Or, is that someone's secret plan for Muslim world domination?

As you read this, decisions will probably already have been made, or bungled, over Iran's atomic bomb program. Or did the clever Iranians convince the world that all those threats and all the secret underground facilities are just to produce a small reactor to power some TV sets? Did Iran's gamble pay off that the Americans would waffle, like they did with North Korean and Pakistani atom-bomb programs … lots of threats but no action?

Did the Israelis and Americans attack, or not? The American military advisors certainly were not deciding. Some analysts imply that the American leaders quaked at the thought that the Iranians, if upset by an attack on their atomic facilities, just might have put some floating mines in the Persian Gulf entrance… the Strait of Hormuz…. which would plug-up THEIR oil tankers going to China as well as those going to America. Was not that threat one of the reasons for America's strategic oil reserve? Oh, right, …. the Europeans don't have much oil reserve. The Russians have been blocking their oil/gas pipelines in mid-winter to annoy the Ukrainians… thereby burning

European oil reserves. Oh, well, ...they can all buy warm woolen underwear. All pulling together, aren't we?

Or, if really annoyed, the fear was… the Iranians may squirt their tanks furiously out onto the Iraqi plain from their western mountain sanctuary and over-run Iraq... and maybe even... shudder... Arabia and the... gasp... American oil wells there! (Yikes! That could DOUBLE gas prices. Would have to cancel our trip!) But aren't those same narrow mountain passes in western Iran the ones that are supposed to stop the American tanks from coming IN to Iran? If the Iranians can block the American tanks in the mountain passes, why can't the Americans block the Iranian tanks? And what happened to all that American air power designed to stop tanks? All that stuff high taxes and deficit financing pay for. Who is doing the thinking here?

And what do the Americans have all those mine-sweepers, helicopters, aircraft carriers and planes sitting there near the Persian Gulf for, ... if not to stop the mine-laying at Hormuz? And if the fearful oil tanker owners can't get insurance policies if Hormuz is threatened, can't the Americans provide insurance? What is all this hand-wringing about, if not President Obama's worry about his image as a 'nice guy'? Well, he did get Bin Laden. Maybe he's changing.

Nevertheless, stopping Iran's illegal nuclear program is not warfare, *it is pollution control!* It will benefit all the world. And if we fail to do that, look at the beginning of Chatper 12... (The One-Day Exchange of 2047) to see how their own nuclear toys may cause their own national suicide … along with the death of millions in China, Korea, Japan, Canada and the USA. Now, there's the true cost of indecision.

And, don't forget.... to an Islamist, the Kor 'an says dying while they are fighting to kill or enslave non-believers is the only certain way to get to heaven... a perpetual paradise! It is the BEST thing they can do. This suicide martyrdom is also the BEST thing they can do for their kids.... that is why we see child-suicide-bombers. Is that why some say Hamas puts missile launchers in schools and hospitals in Gaza.... let the Israelis bomb them... kids who are killed all go to certain paradise... and (is the rumor true?) the parents of the dead kids get huge respect and are paid well from the fund from the American oil payments! And it is interesting how angry the whole world gets at the Israelis, who are accidently sending Muslim kids to paradise. Of course, the kids who are only maimed by the bombs are not so lucky as the dead ones. This terrible situation is the fault of both Israeli and Muslim adults.

Do the people of Iran know the danger of atomic retaliation their government is bringing them? Do they care? And, how about the downwind fallout… does China care? Is no one even a little worried?

*****

The western media has not yet accepted the fact that many Islamist groups are waging war against all non-believers; that after 14 centuries of waiting, now is their big chance to win... to achieve world domination through mass migration. Is it their plan to let the media continue to sleep?

Pakistan

The United States is possibly paying for the production of Pakistani atom bombs that may be used against American people…either by a potentially hostile government in politically unstable Pakistan, or by terrorists who need simply buy the bomb from a hungry Pakistan that needs cash to pay for its rapidly increasing atom bomb inventory… which will soon exceed 200.

Repeat: 200 atom bombs! Why would Pakistan need so many atom bombs when its only enemy is India… and their missiles and planes are limited in range to targets mostly in India? Are they also trying to get longer range missiles to threaten Europe, China or America?

Did the Americans close their eyes while billions in aid money was diverted from food for Pakistani people to build the necessary atomic reactors for the Pakistani atom bomb? Pakistan, in 2011, has three… yes, three! … atomic reactors producing fissionable material (plutonium/uranium) for atom bombs, with a fourth billion-dollar plutonium reactor now under construction (reported in *Newsweek, May 23-30, 2011*) probably with more funds from American aid.

All this at a time Pakistan is begging for financial help for earthquakes and floods that have recently dominated television news in the US.

Dealing with Pakistan...

India is the only country that has the experience to effectively deal with Pakistan, and India will go its own way. Great effort should be made to build friendship between the US and India, since the English language and the desire for prosperity are the great common factors. The US can wisely be an intermediary between Pakistan and India, since the Pakistani military government desperately needs American financial support (even though many poor civilians are Islamist who hate America…and India).

The US should attempt to prevent Pakistan from acquiring missiles that can carry atomic warheads to lands more than 1500 miles distant (only India). The US should try to restrict funds from Pakistan that may be used for more atomic weapons or longer range missiles.

The US should let Pakistan control Afghanistan as they may. The US should withdraw forces from both countries, leaving only well-trained assets (as instructors).

Close monitoring for terrorist activity can be done
by satellite and pilotless drones with Special Forces
follow-up. Similar techniques can be used to monitor
opium-poppy production. The US should become the
prime buyer of raw opium from Afghanistan, destroying
non-medical stocks. Keep prices paid for opium stock as
low as possible, destroying crops surreptitiously where
possible. Offer farmers higher prices to grow non-opium
crops.

    Once ground forces have departed, the US
should support the building of Afghan and Pakistani
infrastructure (roads, bridges, railroads, irrigation
projects, schools and clinics) to bring work and medical
help to the people. Let Pakistan actually deal with the
Taliban. Keep the people there and educate the women
and men to have smaller families. Invest in resource
development. Support and train local leaders to become
national leaders.

Concerning Islam

With all due respect to the Messenger of Allah,
Mohammed (PBUH), to his most excellent representatives
and to all Muslims, rich or poor, and with no intent to
give offense or provoke an angry response, we wish to
include at this time some peaceful suggestions that may
assist all parties in finding peaceful solutions to problems
concerning the continued growth of Islam *(the religion of
peace)* throughout the world.

    Islam is a simple and powerful religion that has the
goal to spread the religion throughout the world as an
all-encompassing religious, social, economic and political
program that uses the ancient 'Sharia' legal system. *Jihad
is* the name given to the forceful *effort of* Muslim people to
extend the power of their religion. There are two difficult-
to-resolve factions in Islam (Sunni and Shia) that have
been at war many times over the past 1400 years. There

are few who even know why there is conflict... other than
extreme intolerance for each other 's views.

The teachings of the Muslim holy book, the God-given
Kor 'an, call for ALL the world to be ruled by a Muslim
Caliph, or King, whose rule is extended by any means,
including war. Since the Kor 'an is accepted by Muslims
to be the actual word of Allah (God), delivered to earth
by the angel Gabriel during the years 610-632 CE through
the unfailing-memory of their illiterate unquestioned
Messenger and Prophet (PBUH), and set onto paper under
the supervision of many learned Arabian scholars shortly
after his ascension to paradise, in 632, the words in the
Kor 'an can be neither questioned nor changed. It is
blasphemy (which carries the death penalty) for anyone
to criticize or ridicule any aspects of the Kor 'an, given
to us all by Allah. The Kor 'an instructs Muslims to
dominate the world and to 'cut the head (off) or enslave' all
non-believers who refuse to submit to the will of Allah (as
interpreted by His Caliph and/or religious leaders).

Islam now has 1.6 billion believers many of whom
who are dedicated to world domination. This is about 50%
more believers than 30 years ago. Islam is the most rapidly
growing major religion, especially in those poor, or less
developed, lands whose willing women happily give their
husbands many children, to more greatly please Allah.

Considering the Above, Non-Believers Can Take Three Possible Actions

1. To submit. This accepts the present 7th Century
   pure and simple Islamic religion, with the
   probability that it will conquer the world through
   its appeal to the poor and the use of its happy
   women to reproduce very many children as
   immigrant-conquerors in all lands of the earth. It is
   hoped that in the future Allah will grant that there
   will be a stop to the internecine warfare between

the followers of Ali (Shia... with a centralized
leadership... mostly in Iran and part of Iraq)
and the 82% traditionalists (Sunni... with local
leadership). Islamic texts stress the Allah-given
perfection of their belief and the total intolerance
of false beliefs and command the destruction or
enslavement of all who refuse to submit to the will
of Allah.

2. To resist. Many Westerners try to see Muslims
in terms of their own egalitarian values... a
fatal mistake. In Islam there is little tolerance
for change. You either believe totally in the one
God Allah and His Messenger Mohammed (PBUH)
and in the teachings of the holy Kor 'an or you
are called an infidel and can be either killed or
enslaved. Historically, some infidels may be
ignored (and heavily taxed)... for awhile. Muslims
must obey the Kor 'an (see below) and their imam
(priest). And there is no changing them. They
can be killed by any Muslim for the crimes of
apostasy or blasphemy if they seek to change their
religion. The answer for non-Muslims: restricting
contact with them, and stopping the movement
of Muslims out of their dominant regions. And
convince (pay) Muslims in foreign lands to return
to their original homes and families. In the long
term... to do whatever is possible to educate and
train young Muslim men and girls in useful skills
to get jobs and in increased tolerance of different
(western) ideas.

Islam is focused on reaching paradise when you
die. Day-to-day life is focused on prayer... more
than on working or how well you are eating. Many
Islamic schools now educate the boys only in the

Kor 'an and other religious subjects, and in hating non- believers ... ignoring employment skills.

The teachers of such schools may be encouraged (paid) to reduce the emphasis on violence toward non-believers and hatred of western values. Other job-oriented educational programs can be encouraged... with students being rewarded for increasing their overall knowledge as well as religious knowledge... with scholarship money going to both students and their parents.

3. Historically, leaders of the Muslim world have used warfare and the mass-murder of non-believers to advance their cause. However, many Muslims believe that their religion is peaceful. Some passages in the holy Kor 'an do not appear to support this… and these passages may encourage some toward violent acts against non-believers. For example, the Arabic word 'jihad' can be interpreted in a spectrum of meanings, from a passive *an effort in some direction* to an aggressive *holy war*. There are thousands of such words with variable meanings.

Given enough time and a less confrontational atmosphere, Islamic scholars may be encouraged to re-examine some of the original Arabic documents to seek wording that is less aggressive and still acceptable to Muslims.

Some examples of direct translations from the Arabic wording in the holy Kor 'an with recent pacified translations for Americans by Prof. Syed Vickar Ahamed: (The Quran. Book of Signs Foundation, 2007, Lombard, Illinois 60148, USA. Third Edition)

> Kor'an: surah 8: 12 "...terrorize the unbelievers.
> strike off their heads and cut off each of their fingers
> and toes."

This present quotation from the holy Kor'an, some
westerners believe, commands or at least encourages
mass-murder of any non-Muslims. Even though the
killing of one non-believer is sufficient to guarantee
paradise for a Muslim who dies in the effort, this
passage in their holy book may have led one US Army
major in 2010 to kill many of his co-workers... and
suicide bombers to kill many more.

Prof. Ahamed translation: Surah 8: 12 (page 92)
"....Give strength to the believers: I will bring about terror
into the hearts of the disbelievers: So you strike above
their necks and hit hard over-all of their finger-tips and
toes."

> Kor'an: surah 47: 4 "...continue carrying out jihad
> against the unbelieving infidels until they submit to
> islam."

Prof. Ahamed's translation for Americans: (page 280)
Surah 47: 4 "Therefore, when you meet the unbelievers
(in battle), strike hard at their necks until you have
completely defeated them. .... But He will never let the
deeds (of) those who are killed in Allah's way be lost."

> Kor'an: surah 9: 5 "Fight and kill the disbelievers
> wherever you find them, take them captive, harass
> them, lie in wait and ambush them"

Prof. Ahamed's translation for Americans: (Page
96) Surah 9: 5 "fight and kill the (distrusted) pagans
wherever you find them, and catch them, attack them,
and stay waiting for them in every stage (of war)"

> Kor'an: surah 4: 95 "allah has granted a higher rank
> to those fighting jihad. he has distinguished his
> fighters with a huge reward."

Prof. Ahamed's translation: (Page 48) Surah 4:95 "... Allah has granted a position higher to those who struggle and fight with their goods and persons than to those who sit (at home). To each Allah has promised good (reward)."

The following quotations are also relevant:

"...suicide bombers of today are the noble successors of their noble predecessors... the most honorable persons among us." Palestinian newspaper **Al-Hayat Al-Jadida, dated 9/11/2001.**

"...it is our religious duty to fight them, including through suicide attacks. The goal is not the killing, but that this is the way to reach Allah. Martyrs have special status in the next world and have bigger chance to watch Allah's face.," a suicide trainee.

✳✳✳✳✳

We have completed our study of the future that included an attempt at defining a better civilization and planning a logical path to that goal. We now recognize the opportunities and the difficulties that lie ahead over the next few centuries. Now we can take some focused action. Failure to strive for and meet the goals that are now clear during the coming Century will not necessarily doom our civilization, but it will make our situation more difficult.

We will certainly have to modify the goals and the plan as current reality requires. We carefully document our plans so we can change them intelligently... hopefully improving them. But planning does not always work. The five-year plans trumpeted by the former Soviet Union did not foresee or prevent its collapse in 1989. The plans made were of the Linear Projection type. We hope that this present BUI method will prove better.

The Grim Predictions of our future still await us. The specter of financial collapse from deficit spending, of civil wars against angry immigrants, of the warmer oceans flooding major cities, of starvation caused by overpopulation and/or failed crops and food distribution, of continued political grid-lock in the US Congress or of the stealthy usurpation of total imperial power by a club of greedy financiers… these are serious problems. But they may not happen. Good leaders can make decisions to reduce or control the dangers. Life does go on.

In ten years, we may look back and laugh about some threats that never materialized. Books on these subjects come and they go. But it is not the function of this book to propose solutions to all these problems. We seek to get past the present to focus on a better future world. While not ignoring these and other threats, we will attempt to distill that which is most important in leading toward the future we have defined.

> **Americans must first recognize their responsibility to the rest of the world to provide calm, mature leadership. this is not a smug assumption of superiority.**

No one person or group of persons is intrinsically better than another. There is no master race. However, some people are luckier than others in where they live. And a lot of people from very different backgrounds have the good luck to live in America. The German poet Goethe put it most simply: "America, you have it better!." Some Americans show disgusting pride and lack of knowledge when they brag that their Italian, Russian, Chinese or Latino parents were better just because they got in the American door. It was the riches of the land that have made so many of its people rich. It is time that golden door be opened to others who would join in the American dream, but not to those who would sabotage it.

And what is the American dream? *We can each be better than we are.*

The essence of our utopia is one world society, without sovereign boundaries. One in which there is little reason for war. But, however small, man will find some justification for war, because it is exciting…. war is his nature… the fiendish pleasure taken in crushing the life out of some helpless victim. The dark side of man… the beast…it is still part of us…. not all of us, but many. One evil man named Hitler did not personally kill all 6 million Jews or all 20 million Russians. Others were also involved. We have even forgotten the million-or-so Gypsies slaughtered. ….Weren't important. Still, they were humans.

We can set up laws, controls and police protections. We can educate… to share common language, values and ideas. We can manipulate. We can build ramparts against our insidious heritage. But we must forever be on guard against ourselves. There will always be the one who will foment a rebellion or a war out of jealousy, revenge…. or just to see if they can do it. There is a reason people wish to be king. Power… over their lives, and others.

So, if we do not commit to a plan to end war, we shall surely continue to have kings, dictators and war.

The first step toward ending war is to begin to end sovereign boundaries. The worst thing we can do is to encourage new empires. For empires are always insular and empires must forever make war, if only to preserve themselves. One unified world means less chance for war. When two great empires divide the world… well, we have been there.

We have already reviewed possible nation-contenders for world leadership. And we have seen only one logical leader, America. But an American military/political empire further dominating the world would only result in eventual rebellion and civil war. While the Americans have the power and prowess, they must be educated and better prepared for responsible leadership. This will take time.

During this time, there will be many other countries sniping at the Americans out of jealousy. But they have no chance at leadership. Will they bring the world to destruction? Or will they help to build our utopia?

While preparing, steps can be taken to begin voluntary political consolidation of the world... without conquest. The logical first place to begin is a political and cultural union of the present nations of Mexico, the United States, and Canada. It will not be easy, but it is necessary. It is hoped that political union will avoid a possible conflict between Latino and Anglo peoples in the western US near the end of this Century. Some unthinking young Latinos actually savor such a conflict to obtain revenge for past offenses.

The successful union of these three North American countries will create a peaceful power base that *MAY* form the nucleus for continued expansion through the continual voluntary union of equal peoples. By this peaceful process, it is envisioned that a world-wide political union of equal peoples may be created in the future. This is not a plan for another empire.

The First Plateau of Goals

To reach the plateau of goals we have set for the first stepping-stone toward our future, the period 2040-70, the United States must begin to demonstrate greater political and economic maturity.... strengthen its culture, its finances and economy, and its political system. The following pages present some of the more obvious challenges. Later we outline an agenda that may meet these challenges.

It is obvious that some of these suggestions will require resources. In 2011 the world economy is unhealthy. It is outside the scope of this project to seek solutions to all short-term problems of government. Irresponsible government, shown recently in the US by both the Executive and Congress, is the cause and the result of problems discussed herein. Most of the plans and programs recommended below must await financing available in an improved national economy…. as well as motivated leadership.

It is also obvious and visible that Canada has solved many of the cultural and financial problems with which the United States is now struggling. Will the US government take some advice from its Canadian brothers?

Lane 1: Cultural A–2016, Protecting Decision-Makers

Very soon, we must protect the government of the United States and the US financial system… and the governments of other great powers….Russia, China, India, Brazil, the UK, Germany, France and others…. from possible atomic (or biological) destruction. With the amount of atomic material now floating around illegally, and the number of oil-rich terrorists trying to get their hands on it, it is possible that in the near future Washington D. C. and New York (possibly Moscow or London) will be hit by an atomic blast or a similar weapon of mass destruction.

This will only be more likely if the Iranians get their atom bomb, since they may already have missiles to carry them… and if they die in a counter-strike after killing millions of infidels, they know they will go immediately to eternal paradise. As a result of such an atomic attack, all federal government functions in Washington and the New York financial activities will stop.

With many or most government officials and financial executives dead or disabled, and with the communication systems down for a long time, one can hardly estimate the chaos that will follow. The fact **that this possibility has so long been ignored is a disgrace approaching criminal negligence.** Major targets simply cannot be fully protected from terrorist attack. By reducing vulnerability, we reduce the likelihood of attack. Deep bunkers inside the city may protect a few, but not enough.

The Executive, the Senate, the Speaker and key Representatives must be gotten to permanent safety outside Washington. All high officials and key congresspersons must be assigned full-time protection and be required to live with their families in a dispersed area at least 15 miles away and up-wind (to the west) from Washington.

The Executive can rule by emergency decree for awhile, but a law-making group of congresspersons must be protected. Members of the same administrative team and of important Senate/House committees must be separated by several miles, using secure water systems and non- interruptible power. A dedicated and secure underground fiber-optic and micro-wave communication system must connect President/vice-president, cabinet members and other executive team members and all senior law- makers... using modern tele-conferencing techniques. Electronic design must consider the effect on electronics of an atomic blast or other disruptive devices.

Laws or administrative decisions must be changed to provide for a quorum of Senators and key Representatives via tele-conferencing. New controls must be developed to reduce the risks of electronic communication. Congressional travel, both overseas and national, must be adjusted to these needs. Families, especially children, of all these officials must also be protected/sequestered with appropriate schooling provided for children and medical services available. Kidnapping is an increasing activity of terrorists. Senators and Executive officers should minimize their physical-time in Washington, and do so on a plan to preserve a quorum of emergency decision-makers.

Most members of the House of Representatives should also move away from Washington and develop a tele-conferencing system that will allow them to function if Washington is destroyed.

While there are now duplicate stock exchange and financial transaction centers outside the New York financial district, these may be inadequate to provide for a continuing finance system should New York's financial district be destroyed. New York is possibly down-wind from Washington, and the fall-out from an atomic blast there would kill/sicken many. New York suburbs, Philadelphia, Hartford and Boston would also be affected. Using tele-conferencing and other secure communications, the executives and key processing personnel (and their families) should be re-located to safety in areas that are outside a likely atomic fallout pattern from Washington or New York. Construction of appropriate secure communications systems (underground) should begin at once. And family fallout shelters with secure water systems should be available for those who may need them.

Hartford and Boston are downwind from New York. The insurance industry in these cities should be likewise dispersed to areas outside main fallout patterns. Insurance calculations should include the above risks, with provision for spreading the risks. The building of fallout shelters in homes down-wind from target areas should be encouraged, with the expense made tax-deductible.

Plans should be begun to relocate the seat of government (New Washington? Federal Center? World City?) to an undersea, possibly mobile, city in the ocean to the east of Virginia or possibly in Lake Eire south of Toronto. Several obsolete aircraft carriers, connected in some way, could begin the ocean project... eventually creating a landing field adequate for medium passenger jets. Two flexible tubes at a depth below wave-action containing people-moving capsules may eventually connect the undersea city with Norfolk. A Lake Eire (or Lake Michigan) location would be more central.

Cultural B: 2020, Population Control

More difficult weather patterns will result in reduced food supplies which will eventually reduce the number of people. Birth rates in many Asian, African and Latin countries continue to be excessively high. Birth rates in many European countries appear to be excessively low. However, population densities in many parts of Europe are high, and a temporary lower birth rate may be responding to a poor economy or to already high densities. Effective government programs can reduce excessive birth-rates. The Thai government succeeded in controlling population growth. The Philippine government did not. The result: an extra 40 million Filipinos in 30 years.

The decision to allow or deny immigration is the right of each country. Many **Americans have forgotten that Presidents Hoover, Truman and Eisenhower forced millions of illegal immigrants to return to their homelands,** in attempts to preserve jobs for local residents during depression and after wars.

No country should be forced to accept angry young immigrants. But Serbia (historically supported by Russia) recently did try to stop Albanians from illegally entering their Kosovo province, only to see the Americans use their military to force the Serbs to give up Kosovo to the new Muslim immigrants. (If the Americans can force a country to give a portion to new immigrants, perhaps the Americans should be forced to do the same with a small state, say, Maryland! Why not New York?)

This showed the Albanian Muslims how to conquer all Europe through immigration. We now see the chaotic results of mass immigration of Muslims into France,

England, Denmark, Belgium and Holland... basically caused by lack of foresight by the geographically uneducated Americans.

Was there a plan to use oil profits to pay the poor Albanians to move across the undefended hills to Kosovo... and Macedonia? Is this a new kind of conquest of American allies financed by American oil money!

Effective controls can stop illegal immigration. That goes for all neighbors of people-exporting lands. But controls are expensive. Friendly (and wise) nations may give support to threatened countries who wish to build effective border controls or necessary border fences. Assistance may be provided for threatened countries to re- build security and military forces that have been infiltrated by unwanted immigrants. Immigration laws may be changed or strengthened.

Advice, encouragement, personal and family protection and financial assistance may be provided to legislators of threatened countries to help them find the courage to pass laws to protect themselves from their violent immigrants. This is part of the cost of freedom. Americans should lead this effort.

Lane 2: Environmental A–2016, Global Warming

The United States should assume world leadership in solving the problem of global warming. The debate over the extent of global warming has been raging for decades. There must now be enough empirical evidence to support government decisions and to identify those persons/companies who have been distorting evidence for financial gain. Either low-lying islands are being submerged or they are not.

Enough time has passed that dependable projections of sea-level change must be available. The polar ice-caps are clearly being reduced. If the seas are indeed rising enough to threaten coastal cities and are due to carbon emissions, we must put in place by 2020 enough improvements in global emissions that the trends will be reversed and the melting of the polar ice cap will have stopped by 2050.

Climate change can be anticipated, and food production and farming techniques adjusted to conform to the new conditions. Farming reform must re-orient some upland farming from beef, milk, hay and fruit production to that of edible grains. Food production, storage and distribution will have to be made more efficient. The teaching of agriculture must be modified to stress the social obligations of farming on a par with the current farming-for-profit agendas. Farming will again become too important to be allowed to fail.

Environmental B: 2020, Weather Forecasting

Weather models must be improved worldwide and distributed to areas where the more extreme weather changes will occur. These models must show estimated weather patterns over several decades for them to be useful.

Insurance programs must be developed so that the risks of farming modifications and population movements by private individuals or companies can be reduced.

Lane 3: Political–Governmental Changes

It is clear that the existing decision-making structures and institutions on the earth are not adequate to plan and control the political adjustments that will be necessary to accommodate the changes of the next Century.

Capitalism and private industry must be preserved because of its proven power to improve mankind. However, overall population reduction and other large changes in human numbers will temporarily require a greater degree of central planning and control than we now have. We realize that poor planning in the past has given the process a bad name. We must improve. Also required will be an increase in the quality and foresight of our leaders that can only come from a greatly improved world educational system, and in the methods we use to select our leaders.

Leadership is the subject of many books and educational programs. The American high school program of the Reserve Officer's Training Corps (ROTC) is a noted success. The families of leaders tend to acquire wealth, which is passed on to children through access to the best schools and teachers, as well as through family investments. Potential leaders who are less wealthy tend to be ignored. Improved educational information systems should identify and assist those persons.

It is certain that greater use of information technology will be needed to provide controls in the more complex political systems of the future, and the use of mass psychology will be necessary if large highly reproductive populations are to be convinced to have fewer children.

Historical methods of political leader selection are clearly inadequate. Constitutions may be amended to increase the age and relevant experience levels of leader-candidates. A training period of adequate time can be required before elected leaders can assume full power.

Protections against the illegal usurpation of power can be increased. And power-conspiracies may be anticipated and made more visible to the public by a computer-control model. Eventually we seek a steady-state political system where few new laws are required and there may be less urgency for powerful leadership. This will be the time to reduce the cost and complexity of government.

Political A: By 2017

The demands of the American Presidency are clearly greater than the strengths and abilities of any one person. Too many important matters compete for the attention of the leader. Some must be ignored, only to become explosive demands of the future. This forces a President to be a 'fireman', rather than a leader, and frustrates the plans of the best person.

As a beginning, a President may now appoint three well-qualified assistants and delegate to them powers to act in his name to reduce the burden of political and organizational activities while the President focuses on planning and policy. Full-time Congressional liaison can be delegated to one of these persons, the Commander-in-Chief function to another, and cabinet liaison to another (this is the one who goes out in Air Force One to fly over natural disasters, and who meets with foreign dignitaries). These persons should work in one private office and maintain contact in daily meetings. Adjacent meeting rooms would supplement tele-conferencing. An adequate small information system can support their schedules and programs… and record results.

Political B: By 2017

Steps should be begun to bring together the governments and peoples of Mexico, the US and Canada. This is in addition to the already implemented 'North American Free Trade Area'. Strong resistance to a closer political relationship must be expected from both Mexico and Canada… who take pride in their sovereignty.

Canada, in particular, would bring great cultural and human benefits to a union with the United States, as well as huge natural resources. A voluntary equal partnership between the two countries would benefit both, but the United States should be prepared to act the role of a generous suitor in wooing the Canadians. The Canadians will benefit also, but the United States will benefit more… and should therefore do whatever is necessary to encourage a political bond between the two nations. French and maritime Canada must participate fully in all negotiations, and full respect and consideration must be given to the needs of the autonomous Inuit peoples of the arctic region. The Canadian people have historical reasons for distrusting their erstwhile southern neighbors. The time has come to address those reasons, with whatever effort and resources it will take.

Mexico, possibly retains much resentment for abusive treatment by the American military in the past, especially the slaughter of many students during the 1847 American conquest of Mexico City (long forgotten by most Americans who do not study history.... OK, one easy semester in junior High School. Really enough?). Amends must be made by Americans. It is useless to re-construct the details of actions taken in a one-sided war that occurred over 165 years ago. But Mexicans have not forgotten nor forgiven. The French (under Napoleon III) may share some blame here. If the United States wishes to create a political unity with Mexico, the US should address this issue with justice and sensitivity... including expressing some regret for obvious excesses.

Greatly increased investment in Mexico should be accompanied with equally increased financial and educational aid to Mexico, especially in the area of English as a Second Language. The five-year goal should be 4 years of English taught to every Mexican student. Spanish is already taught in the majority of American high schools. This should be increased with improved quality, along with the teaching of the Chinese language. Language instruction belongs in the first years of schooling, not the last.

Much more effort must be made to build friendship and understanding among all peoples of the Mexican-American southwest US. And appropriate measures must be taken to reduce resentment that lingers over US treatment of Mexicans during the past two centuries.

The United States needs a political and cultural bond with the Mexican people to enable the enlarged union to provide effective leadership on the world stage. Americans must do MORE than their share to build a voluntary equal partnership with the Mexican people.

It must be anticipated that the very wealthy leading families of Mexico, including some of the newly rich, will have many doubts about, if not hostility, to the idea of political union with the United States. It may take generations and much generosity to satisfy them. This also includes negotiations with drug lords.

Mexican immigrants, legal and illegal, should be given permanent resident status in the United States. And they should be strongly encouraged and assisted to depart the southwest and migrate to the US northeast and Canada, where they are needed and should be welcomed. Their beautiful culture can make a great contribution to that of all north America and the world.

Latinos should be paid to learn English. It will be an excellent investment. Increasing their effectiveness in the United States will benefit all Americans. Those Mexicans who are agricultural or factory workers must be given special assistance and access to learning. Small portable computers may be a solution.

This may also be the place to encourage the United States to strongly assist students at all levels in the Philippines and in Poland to learn English.

Political C: By 2017

The President should put in place a plan to examine scenarios for the future. This plan should contain provisions of improved relations with world powers with the goal of maintaining peace. It is about time we learned to share. The entire question of maintaining a balance of power in various world regions to protect American interests should be re-examined. The policy does not fit with the new world-role of the United States envisioned here.

In particular, the US should cooperate with Russia in that country's effort to stabilize and defend its borders and maintain its traditional sphere of influence. The United States is NOT in the best position to evaluate and solve geopolitical problems in the Russian region. All effort must be made to eliminate or solve areas of potential military conflict, which would benefit no one.

The US should try to re-build the friendship, through cooperation and financial assistance, with the peoples of the European Union. Special emphasis should be placed on relations with Britain, Germany, France and Poland. Active assistance should be offered by the Americans in their dealing with immigrant problems.

Political D: By 2017

Persons from Muslim-dominated homelands who are legally in America must be encouraged (generously paid) to return to their homelands. Those who choose to remain must obey American laws and adjust their behavior, and that of their families, to fit into the American culture. Those who are not American citizens should be quickly deported under legal processes. The Muslim Kor 'an and other texts teach that good Muslims must forever try to dominate all other religious groups… this is not compatible with American religious freedom. Persons who choose to leave the Muslim religion must be protected from religious- murder by other Muslims. Immigration and unnecessary visits to the US by persons from the Muslim world should be discouraged. Americans must await such time as Muslims change to tolerate American religious freedom and their Constitution without trying to destroy them both.

When will Americans notice that many Muslim groups have declared war on them? Do Americans think

Muslims will change their minds and apologize? Must Americans tolerate enemies in their own land?

Political E: By 2017

Friendly relations with China must be given renewed emphasis. Financial assistance should be given to China to greatly expand English as a second language in schools. The teaching of Chinese in the US should be expanded. Expanded American university offerings must be made available to Chinese students both in America and in China. Close financial cooperation should be maintained with our Chinese friends without constant political heckling. Americans must be taught that Chinese cultural problems are different, and Chinese methods of dealing with them must be respected.

A policy of cooperation should be established by the US in meeting China's needs for expanded resources. The US Navy should actively assist all Chinese merchant shipping on the high seas. The US should also cooperate (not compete) with China on space exploration and moon landings.

Political F: By 2017

The countries of Brazil and India should receive special attention in terms of increased friendship, educational and economic assistance, exchange of students, expanded American university admissions and joint research projects. English as a second language should receive expanded assistance in both countries.

Political G: By 2030

Great progress must have been made in satisfying the needs of the large Spanish-speaking group of people in the western U.S. Strong incentives, such as financial assistance, education, transportation and job relocation assistance must be offered to those persons who will

relocate to areas of less-dense Latino population.
Governmental policies must be changed in favor of
greater integration of Spanish-speaking persons into the
larger Amerimexican community. Again, non-English-
speaking Latinos in north America must be paid to learn
to speak and read English.

Political H: By 2030

Americans should have strengthened their Constitution,
created stronger governmental control over the financial
sector, created a stronger Office of the Presidency, and
continued in monitoring the international operations of
American corporations to increase responsible behavior
and increase sensitivity to the needs of other peoples.

The US Constitution must be updated and prepared
for a more universal role on this planet as well as with
future extra-terrestrial colonies. This may be accomplished
through judicious constitutional amendments. An entirely
new US constitution would be a potential disaster,
polluting the purity of the existing document with pages
of political argot, legal obfuscation and excessive detail
designed by lawyers and other 'political experts' to
weaken the basic protection of the Constitution against
kings and dictators.

Many more recent constitutions, while claiming to
emulate that of the United States, are weak documents
that pander to the masses and breed corruption. They
posit supreme power to lie with the people rather than
in the Constitution itself, thereby inviting the chaos of
the ancient 'pure democracy'. They permit changes in
the basic laws to be made far too easily. Even worse, they
are filled with detailed rules to satisfy different pressure
groups that should be the province of legislated laws
and executive decisions. They often do not provide for a
strong judicial review of new laws to insure conformance
with the existing Constitution.

A review of several national constitutions that were supposedly based on the US Constitution reveals how professional politicians and 'legal experts' can weaken and distort a constitution to the point that it no longer protects the people from the rule of a king or dictator.

The Russian Constitution obviously fails to prevent one man (Putin) from becoming a life-time boss... allowing him to rotate between the President and Prime Minister positions... both of which must have nearly equal power. Normally, in a Prime-ministerial system the office of President (Head of State) is a prestigious but low-power ceremonial position for an elder statesman as compared with the powerful Prime Minister who is leader of the strongest political party and Head of the Government (the chief lawmaker).

The German 'Basic Law' constitution (of 1987) panders to the still occupying powers, posits weakly the supremacy of 'the people' rather than in itself, provides only the most casual judicial review of new laws to insure conformity to itself, and bases the political stability of the entire country on the whim of a small electorate that happens to be the home of the Chancellor (Prime Minister).

The Philippine Constitution again vaguely places 'supreme authority' in the people (easily swayed by a popular dictator) rather than in itself, makes changes too easy, has very uncertain judicial review of new laws and is filled with pages of detailed social rules and 'should be' laws that are mere populist platitudes and guarantees that should be put in place through legislation.

The supreme power of the written US Constitution is rare among the basic laws of the countries in the world. Its simplicity and understandability are nearly unique. We must protect this document from radical change.

States and Provinces of both Mexico and Canada may be admitted as States to an Amerimexican Union without changing the present US Constitution. This would make the political units of Mexico and Canada equal to each of the States of the present United States. However, an amendment to the US Constitution would be needed to upgrade it to having supreme authority for the entire Amerimexican Union, along with adaptations to fit it geographically to the entire world. Merely changing the words "United States" to "Amermexican (or Northamerican) Union" may suffice to upgrade many of the existing articles in the present Constitution of the United States. Other very limited amendments to wording would also be needed, such as changing the term President to 'Office of the President'.

The existing States of Mexico and the USA, along with the Provinces of Canada together make up between 90 and 100 political units which would fit into the definition of Representative Districts in the World Union political system herein defined. Eventually, a union of all of North America may be facilitated by combining the group of 90-100 'Districts' into between 12 and 15 North American Provinces (as defined in this book) which would provide delegates to the future World Senate (which when complete will consist of around 125 Provinces representing the entire world).

Summarizing part of Chapter 7, the approximately 125 world Provinces would each elect two Senators to the World Senate. The 90 -100 smaller 'Districts' in North America would be slowly restructured (similar to present re-districting) into about 150 population groupings (now called Representative Districts), each with about 2 to 3 million voters. Eventually, each of the approximately 1000 Representative Districts in the world would elect a man and a woman Representative to the approximately 2000 member World House of Representatives… which will be the main law-making body for the entire World Union.

Again, the 2000 member World House of
Representatives would be linked to their approximately 3
billion world voter/constituents by the Voter Information
System and many political messengers (Escorts).

The resulting political system would be stronger and
more stable than the present Presidential system of the
United States with some of the features of the English
Prime-ministerial system. .. with better checks and
balances than either.

To Review...

The 3-member Office of the President would be elected
for overlapping terms by the World Senate from members
of the World Executive Committee. The 28 member
World Executive Committee is composed of a male and
female leader elected from each of the thirteen Regions of
the world plus two added Americans, plus the 3 voting
Presidents. They are elected from senior members of
the World Senate by members of the World Senate and
Houses of Representatives.

Members of the World Senate (1 male and one
female) are elected directly by popular vote of each of
the world's approximately 123 Provinces. The 13 Regions
have bi-cameral legislatures elected by popular vote
from the Political Districts in each Region. The World
House of Representatives has one male and one female
Representative from each of the approximately 1,000
world Political Districts.

This system permits the top executive (Presidential)
level to focus on policy with the advice of the World
Executive Committee, which is itself elected by and from
the members of the World Congress. At the level of the
World Congress, direct responsiveness to the voters must
be maintained. There can be expected that political parties
will influence all decisions. The Constitution may limit the

number of political parties to five, or those which attain ten-percent of votes in a particular Province.

Political I: By 2040

The United States must be far advanced in negotiations for full and equal political union with Canada and Mexico. This will defuse a potential future internal conflict with future Mexican majorities in many areas of the US southwest.

It must be expected that population flows from Mexico into the US territories will increase temporarily when such union begins. These people should be directed to the US east. Massive investment by the United States must be made in Mexican infrastructure, education and industry. This may be similar to the massive investment made in the former land of East Germany by the people and government of West Germany.

As wages rise and living conditions improve in Mexico, population movements northward will slow, then stop. Most Anglo-Americans have little knowledge of the cultural and mineral riches that are Mexico. The time has come to teach them.

Of course, the present Mexican drug culture must be corrected by building a drug barrier around Mexico as well as the present US and using the military to enforce drug laws… and by making drug usage by all Amerimexicans less interesting. Those in Mexico that gain huge profits from drug trade must be somehow convinced to stop.

It is true that marijuana can destroy people, as can alcohol and tobacco. Either ban them all or allow them all… and tax them all a lot.

Political J: Period 2025–2045

Design work completed on the Information Technology part of the Voter Information System which will be the heart of the political structure of the future.

Key decisions relating to technical design will be the types of data bases and the nature of the input-output communication devices which will be integral in the system. It is too early to estimate data bases and user devices that will be available when the system is implemented (perhaps in the 2060 decade).

However, we can look at some possible communication examples which such design may embody:

Sample communications of the Voter Information System to a Voter:

- 'From Rep. Chan on 2 May 2095. Escort John Brooks is ready to explain both sides of question to increase tax rate for barley water.'
- 'From Rep. Chan on 7 July '95. Barley water tax increased 2%.'
- Thank you for your positive vote. Pos. Vote: 156,465, Neg. Vote: 122,486 Certified by auditor R. Peters–#7849.'
- Your Escort John Brooks wishes you a fine birthday.'
- 'From Rep. Chan on 16 Aug 2095. Your New Field refund has been sent to your bank account ending in ###7483.'
- 'Storm warning from Escort John Brooks Sept. 5. Winds of 180 km expected Sept. 6 with flooding.'
- 'From Rep. Chan. Your appl. for damage claim submitted by Escort J. Brooks on 2 Oct. 2095.'

Lane 4: Education

Education reform is the key to our future. Government funded research must be increased to provide incentives to universities to take the lead in the many research projects required.

The present custodial (baby-sitting) function of elementary and middle schools must be changed. An entirely new system of education must be developed that emphasizes the teaching of employable skills and international leadership talent. The British model of education should be examined as a world standard, since it has produced many students with skills in political-geography, world history, languages and leadership... as well as math and sciences.

The present rigid system of union control that prevents the replacement of poor teachers in the United States must be changed through parental pressure and courageous legislative action. How can we continue to allow our children's education to be ruined by incompetent or uncaring teachers?

Education A: By 2017

All students in America must prove their proficiency in English or take and pass English language courses, even if they speak other languages in their homes or jobs.

All persons coming to the United States on student visas should be required to pass the Test of English as a Foreign Language **and be assigned a friendly and trained companion to assist them in their relocation to this country.** We must assure that persons who study in the United States do not go away angry. Deans in colleges must be taught not to neglect groups of foreign students or individuals. All foreign students must be actively encouraged to learn, accept and participate in American cultural and social activities.

By 2018 all persons migrating to the United States must be assisted to read and speak some English. Great improvements can be made in developing different levels of English communication. All persons do not need to be English scholars.

Serious research work must have begun to simplify the English language and make it easier to learn for all. This job cannot be left entirely to academics, since theirs is a world of competitive complexity, not simplicity.

The U.S. Department of Education must mandate improvements in the teaching of world economic geography, so that future Americans will be better acquainted with world problems and potential. We have had enough of ill-prepared presidents. Future world leaders from the US must represent American power, but understand the entire world.

Lane 5: Economics, The Problem

The problem with the American economy is that many voters may have lost confidence in the honesty of the Congress. Do the members of the Congress think that the average voter is stupid and cannot detect lies? This question is posed by a recent very false attack advertisement on television… that showed an elderly lady being thrown off a cliff to give the impression that the opposing party wishes to reduce benefits to older voters. At election time, do they believe that big money for television advertising will confuse the voters enough that the incumbents will probably be re-elected? And so they continue to act in their own best short-term financial interest, even cynically giving themselves benefits that are denied all voters… and continuing to ignore serious threats against the nation's economy.

> **The best check on an incompetent congress is an effective executive, a President who will provide leadership and demand honest behavior from the members of congress.**

Economics A: 2012

The President must slowly re-build world confidence in the American economic system. The dominance of major financial institutions must be brought under the control of law. Existing laws must be more strongly enforced.

2016–Taxes must be increased on gasoline in order to reduce dependency on Muslim oil and to reduce air pollution. Gasoline in the United States costs about half that in many countries of the world. This is the cause of US dependence on Muslim oil and the source of Muslim riches which finance Muslim immigration and jihad. How often must our Congress be reminded of this?

Means must be found to reduce the national debt. Again, the US may wisely follow the lead of the Canadians.

Even if most forces can be withdrawn from Iraq and Afghanistan, highly mobile forces should be in the area to assist these countries in protecting themselves. Money may be saved by reducing present heavy armored divisions, artillery battalions and heavy bomber wings that are focused on obsolete Cold War tactics.

For multi-tribal countries like Afghanistan, rather than attempting full control by military forces, it would seem possible to prevent the establishment of terrorist bases by closely monitoring all activity in a country with a combination of satellite and aerial drone observation along with secret local (native) observers who can call for special force teams as needed. Drug production can be limited by destroying crops and paying farmers to grow other crops. It is obvious that these programs must be established with great care.

Lane 5: Language & Religion A, 2018

The United States should take the lead in making the English language simpler and more easily taught at three or four levels of competence for different users. This project could be contracted with a firm of language experts, who already have good tools. Once an improved language and teaching tools are available, they should be subsidized to expand English learning globally. Language is the chief problem relating to a world government.

Lane 5: Language & Religion B, 2020

The defense against radically militant political-religions will dominate international relations for generations. Islam may overwhelm the West, or it may be held in check, but it will not go away.

The only way to protect non-Muslim peoples from militant Islam is to separate Muslims from non-Muslims. Muslims must be encouraged to remain in their own homelands… restrained from entering or settling in the non-Muslim world… and their ability to attack non-Muslims must be limited, until some time in the future if or when they choose to remove aggressive politics from their religion.

The Czech Republic may be paying Muslim people in their midst to return to their homelands. This policy should be closely examined.

World Systems: By 2050

Political union with Canada and Mexico should be accomplished and in the final stages of implementation.

The first steps toward political and economic union with several other countries should have been taken. A plan must be made that will consider all aspects of this project, which cannot be done under the auspices of the presently constituted United Nations organization (which is too weak). The United Kingdom, The Irish Republic (Eire), Sweden and Poland might be among the first candidates for full partnership with the North American Union in an effort to create an effective world government. These states would eventually become part of a North European political region in a world union.

Space Systems: By 2050

The North American Commonwealth (or the Amerimexican Union), in equal partnership with China, will have at least one major space station orbiting the earth. The station will have manufacturing facilities as well as fabrication units involved in putting new energy systems in place. Provision will be made for some retirement apartments for those who can afford them. The station will be a major trans-shipment facility (as in the movie *2001–a Space Odyssey*) for a new facility on the surface and under the surface of the moon.

The moon facility will also have manufacturing provisions and a food-growing and water-producing ability. Much effort will go into expanding underground caverns for eventual use as controlled-atmosphere cities and/or farms. The mining of high-value metals will have begun, with residences on-site for some mining families.

✳✳✳✳✳

A Presidential commission may expand and refine the above preliminary listing of important projects for the Century 2015–2115. This is the period of greatest risk of war, as different countries resist or cooperate in the huge changes that must be made.

Sooner or later the concept of national sovereignty must disappear in favor of one world government.

There is, in 2014, a group of countries who say they are practicing representative democracies but who have governments which dominate, manipulate and abuse the trust of their people in favor of an entrenched dictator or a group of wealthy families who seek only increased riches at the expense of a majority of poor people. These

'Aristocratic democracies' (ruled by a small group of rich families) are in many cases feudal societies which are based on the near-enslavement or financial domination of most of their peoples to service their limitless greed. These governments are basically unstable and corrupt and often lead to armed revolutions which affect other countries. The dominant families will possibly fight very strongly against a world-government which will limit their avarice. The Amerimexican Union can strongly encourage, or force, change.

The Amerimexican Union Is Our Only Hope For A Future Without War

There is simply no other political/cultural combination on earth that will have enough power to deal with all the problems. It will not be easy. Americans may even have to do some long-range thinking…

They show a lack of wisdom when they think one country has to 'best' another, to 'win' this or that cold war, or that either party must dominate Congress. Chaos! All lose! What has happened to compromise? Aren't Democrat and Republican elected representatives paid by the people of the US to compromise for the benefit of all? Winning and losing are so absurdly temporary. Teenagers think that winning and losing are important. Adults know they are the same. We are all in the same country. We are all on the same small planet. Why make people hate us? We are stuck with each other forever.

Americans need to do whatever is necessary to forge a union of equal partners with Canadians and Mexicans, and make it turn into simply a single union. **Stop worrying about giving-away the store. It's all in the family!**

14

AN AGENDA

This program needs your help, or the help of any enthusiastic person who can improve and sell it to other influential persons.

The only progress toward the goals of this book will come through the efforts US citizens at the grass-roots level, using the internet and other social media.

It is reasonable to expect a delay of perhaps several years before an adequate ground-swell of citizen support in America can find a political voice strong enough to be noticed by the fractious US congress. It will take even longer before a President will feel compelled to lead the project. The leadership of a President is important.

Due to the bashing we have taken in Iraq and Afghanistan, it would be surprising for the US to get involved in any wars during the next few years. There may even be a reduction in US forces, since congress appears to be blind to the Islamic threat. Iran, Russia and China may take advantage of the US 'burned fingers' and congressional inaction to pursue their possibly conflicting agendas.

America can start a policy of friendly cooperation on the high seas… assisting all foreign, especially chinese, shipping in time of need. this may reduce

pressure on the chinese to expend great resources
to build an un- necessary competing navy.

While the strongest possible stance must be taken
against the very real threat from iran, it would seem
a more passive attitude with russia must be taken.
russian leader Putin needs time to rebuild russian
strength, and his authoritarian approach may be
just what the russian people desire... until they
are more ready for the stresses of representative
democracy.

The long-term nature of this book obviously places
it outside the scope of short-term fixes to erroneous
policies in government spending and other
financial problems, as well as recent short-sighted
geopolitical decisions. the next few years will be
especially challenging.

There may be civil war in at least one European country
in the next 20 years, as locals try to expel immigrants and
immigrant-filled security forces fail to keep peace. France
and Holland, possibly Belgium, are going to have much
trouble. The failure of any European state will result in a
metastasizing cell of radical Islam in the heart of Europe,
which might collapse the European Union. America is
usually drawn into European conflicts. A wise American
President will establish whatever foreign policy necessary
to prevent civil war in Europe

During The Near-Term

As soon as an American President or Secretary of State (or
chairman of Senate Foreign Relations) is able to support
the improved plan based on this book, quiet discussions
can begin with the President of Mexico and the Prime
Minister of Canada to explore mutual interests in eventual
political union. This can be built upon from the existing

Free Trade Area. Due to the historical bullying of the United States, much suspicion and even hostility can be expected from Mexicans. However, the benefits of union for both nations would be huge… as long as this union occurs before such time as large groups of Muslims have implanted themselves in Mexico. They are trying. Many Mexicans have lost their Catholic fervor and may be open to the simplicity of Islam… especially if Muslims support anti-American ideas.

Leading To The 2020 Us Election

US Congressional gridlock can be expected to continue until a majority of all parties is pressured by aroused voters to support some world-view program similar to that in this book. One might hope this could occur before the 2020 election. While some changes may be effected through legislation, the resulting laws would probably be weak compromises and therefore inadequate to correct present weakness in the American system. Part of this plan may be implemented by Presidential decision. Eventually constitutional amendments will be needed, as long as the process does not include a general Constitutional convention, which may destroy the basic strengths of the United States. Only after new laws or constitutional articles are in place can real progress be made.

By 2030

Political union agreements with Mexico and Canada may possibly be in place by 2030. It is impossible to predict how this movement may affect the ongoing process in Europe of expulsion of unwanted immigrants.

While local civil war may threaten in some European countries, it is hoped that wise politicians will be able to achieve a more stable society without bloodshed. Future immigration policy must be stronger, to insure that immigrants become productive and accepted citizens, rather than resentful outcasts, and immigrants must be distributed thinly throughout the native society. The process will cost a lot of money, and result in countries with a shortage of labor in jobs that were once filled by expelled immigrants. Factories are already moving to countries with excess labor, instead of labor immigrating to the jobs. Citizens must be prepared (educated) to understand and accept higher living costs associated with the loss of cheap immigrant labor. Also, immigration policy may be adjusted to admit persons from a variety of world cultures and non-political religions... and encouraging their rapid local integration and dispersion.

It can be expected that population movement and cultural problems from the Amerimexican union will persist for a generation. Insurrections can be expected in Mexico, as well as sabotage from wealthy landlords who now consider large sections of Mexico to be their private family fiefdoms.

Spanish (and French) language skills will be demanded of plan promoters.

During this time educational reform and language design efforts must proceed in tandem with political union. The power and prestige of the Amerimexican Union may motivate teachers to begin improvements and overcome resistance to language comonalization. A ten- year research contract (carefully avoiding dominance by overly-zealous academic scholars) may be adequate to discover the path to a true world language.

The Time Block Between 2020 and 2040 Will Be the Most Crucial Dealing With European Islamization

Further progress on world union will depend on the outcome of this process.

This will also be the time of improvement of Constitutions.... and beginning the effort to eliminate rich- family feudalism in many countries… including Mexico. It will also be the time of economic design… to insure the viability of small business in a world of giant firms.

Beginning About 2050, Colonies On Space Platforms and Perhaps The Moon…

The great space adventure begins.

Adding further complexity to the Union-building process, after mid- Century we can expect solar-system exploration and settlement to begin in earnest. If China or India have not yet chosen to participate in the World Union, accommodation must be made to encourage joint partnerships in space to prevent competition between these great nations and the incipient World Union.

By Year 2060

Once the Amerimexican Union is a stable fact, talks may begin with carefully selected nations that may wish to join the Union as equal partners, with the goal of eventual union of most countries in the world. Among those countries which may be first considered are Great Britain, Eire, Poland, Australia and New Zealand. It should be clear by now that political union with the North-American group will be accomplished by admission of new states as Provinces in the Amerimexican Union… which can be expected to become an eventual World Union. These new Provinces will be equal to all other Provinces in the Union, but the existing Constitution in itself will remain supreme in its power with no equal.

Each joining country will present a unique set of problems, which can only be worked out with time. Only when all countries in a new group have achieved comfort in the new union can a new group of countries be considered. It is probable that the countries comprising the North European Region and the Pacific Basin Region may be brought into the Union as a group.

World Language... Development and Implementation, About 2050-70

The problem of language, especially between giant China and the probable English-speaking World Union will be very complex. Further details are outside the present scope of this work. The new electronic social media will have a large impact on this problem.

Time Period 2060 To About 2150...

An optimistic schedule of union-building may envision 50 percent of the approximately 180 countries on the globe to be a part of the World Union within these periods. Since other countries will be preparing, and unique problems of cultural bonding may become routine, the final 45 percent of countries may achieve entry into the Union within the fifty-year period 2130–2180. By this time the new world political system will have been installed and tested.

Great progress must also be made in cultural improvements such as re-designing cities to be more livable, reversing ocean pollution and setting up cost-effective counseling programs in all regions to help people find employment and personal life satisfactions.

2160–2190

The final five percent of countries may take more decades to make necessary modifications to permit entry into the World Union. These may be very difficult, with a tangible risk of civil insurrection that will have to be carefully handled. In addition, there may be rebellious or recalcitrant groups or districts which simply cannot abide World Union, and must be isolated and monitored until such time as their cultures change.

During this entire period of Union-building there will be a tangible risk of political, economic, or cultural conflict or collapse which must be monitored and controlled by a tactful and highly motivated group of civil servants in the new World Union. Those persons are of crucial importance, and their training and indoctrination must begin now... and never end.

It is during this time that major language standardization can take place. A trained group of speakers of any new language or improved world-language will have had time to penetrate society and begin acceptance efforts.

Language development and education is an art that will be so heavily impacted by technology that it is difficult to imagine such in the 2160s. Implanted very small computers or other communication devices using enhanced brain telepathy may so change language and speech that feelings and meaning can be transmitted without words using a standardized icon language. The implications are terrifying.

15

THE DECADE 2540–50, HELL

How Could It Happen?

Three hundred years ago, in 2200, we had everything. We had built ourselves a real utopia, because we did it right. And we thought it would last.

Remember the I-phone? … that little hand-held computer with tiny color screen that addicted so many about 500 years ago, in 2015. It enabled an entirely new form of pure democracy throughout the world. Everyone could speak to everyone, without shouting. Photos and short-movie-clips instantly to anywhere. But eventually everyone became saturated with so many images and messages that they all stopped paying attention. Emotional isolation in a raging sea of information began to increase the rate of suicide. We had built some warning systems, but they were ignored. We continued to develop the social media technology as a utopian goal in itself.

It all seemed so logical. So delightful. But, of course, we had forgotten about the BUI planning thing back in 2250, once we had achieved our utopia. It all seemed so good. We just let normal linear development move us on into an accidental future… enjoying the new toys and marvels that the science system produced.

The cursed breakthrough occurred when they finally got 100 linked computer-systems each with the power of ten I-phones down to the size of one cubic millimeter.

Some saw the danger. Governments tried to set up rules to prevent implantation of the tiny computers into humans. But it happened anyway. Some foolish genius figured out how to attach that tiny super-I-phone-computer inside the head to the human optic nerve. Wow! All that power and information displayed directly into the brain cortex whenever you wanted to close your eyes. They even were able to see the display with open eyes, but most people were content to spend most of the day with their eyes closed to get the better display color … surrounded and entranced by their new electronic environment …. and with trained dogs to lead them where they wanted to go. The new implanted computer toy was simply too addictive. Education stopped. Who needed it?

Those who were rich were able to replace organs with cyborg-electronic parts. China made the cheapest. Life was extended indefinitely. The wealthy became nearly immortal… part computer-hybrid. It was wonderful. The poor and those in backward areas missed-out. Luckily.

Then, they connected the brain-I-phone-system to the electronic toys they developed in the 2200s that extended the video-game sight and sound sensations to all the senses. This caused an explosion of ecstasy all over the body. It was better than heroin. Totally addictive. Why be bothered with sex? Reproduction dropped ninety percent and populations plummeted.

At the same time the Moon-colony and the Neptune colony revolted. Their needs had been neglected by the pre-occupied World Union on planet earth. Since defensive rocket launching from strong-gravity earth displayed a huge heat bloom, all Earth-defenses had to be pre-set in space around the moon, and since rockets launched from the moon left almost no heat flash, Earth-defenses were quickly disabled… leaving the earth-planet defenseless.

The solar system became a hornet's nest of hostile planetary colonies, each threatening the other with instant annihilation. All humans on earth moved underground… into sealed caves… and man-made caverns.

Once again, cave-men. The Castle? Lost.

End.

ABOUT THE AUTHOR

Jules Verne, in 1870, wrote novels about modern submarines and moon rockets. Professor Kaiser here creates a plan for a peaceful world civilization based on present and coming technology. In building these ideas he has worked and traveled in 119 countries on six continents.

His degrees are from Duke University, Univ. of Hawaii and UMASS. He was a USAF missile officer, a supervising management consultant for the largest international accounting firm and a teacher in Hong Kong, Germany, New York and California.

Dr. Richard W. Kaiser
kaiser44441@gmail.com

www.ingramcontent.com/pod-product-compliance
Lightning Source LLC
Chambersburg PA
CBHW050441290526
45786CB00006B/2108

* 9 7 8 1 5 0 3 3 0 2 1 7 4 *